John Dryden

The Works of Virgil

The ninth book auf the Aeneis

John Dryden

The Works of Virgil
The ninth book auf the Aeneis

ISBN/EAN: 9783742895158

Manufactured in Europe, USA, Canada, Australia, Japa

Cover: Foto ©Thomas Meinert / pixelio.de

Manufactured and distributed by brebook publishing software
(www.brebook.com)

John Dryden

The Works of Virgil

THE

WORKS

OF

VIRGIL.

VOL. IV.

THE

WORKS

OF

VIRGIL:

TRANSLATED INTO

ENGLISH VERSE

By Mr. DRYDEN.

VOLUME the FOURTH.

LONDON:

Printed for C. BATHURST, J. RIVINGTON and
T. CASLON, J. ROBSON, B. LAW, G. ROBINSON,
T. CADELL, J. JOHNSON, J. MURRAY, R.
BALDWIN, J. DEBRETT, W. FLEXNEY, T. EVANS,
and J. MACQUEEN.

M DCC LXXXII.

THE

NINTH BOOK

OF THE

ÆNEIS.

THE

ARGUMENT.

*TURNUS takes advantage of Æneas's abfence,
fires fome of his fhips, (which are transformed into
fea-nymphs) and affaults his camp. The Trojans re-
duc'd to the laft extremities, fend Nifus and Euryalus
to recal Æneas; which furnifhes the poet with that
admirable epifode of their friendfhip, generofity; and
the conclufion of their adventures.*

The Ninth Book of the

Æ N E I S.

WHILE thefe affairs in diftant places pafs'd,
    The various Iris Juno fends with hafte,
To find bold Turnus, who, with anxious thought,
The fecret fhade of his great grandfire fought.
Retir'd alone fhe found the daring man;   5
And op'd her rofy lips, and thus began.
What none of all the gods cou'd grant thy vows;
That, Turnus, this aufpicious day beftows.
Æneas, gone to feek th' Arcadian prince,
Has left the Trojan camp without defence;   10
And, fhort of fuccours there, employs his pains
In parts remote to raife the Tufcan fwains:
Now fnatch an hour that favours thy defigns,
Unite thy forces, and attack their lines.

This faid, on equal wings fhe pois'd her weight, 15
And form'd a radiant rainbow in her flight.

The Daunian hero lifts his hands and eyes;
And thus invokes the goddefs as fhe flies.
Iris, the grace of Heav'n, what pow'r divine
Has fent thee down, thro' dufky clouds to fhine? 20
See they divide; immortal day appears;
And glitt'ring planets dancing in their fpheres!
With joy, thefe happy omens I obey;
And follow to the war, the god that leads the way.

Thus having faid, as by the brook he ftood, 25
He fcoop'd the water from the cryftal flood;
Then with his hands the drops to Heav'n he throws,
And loads the pow'rs above with offer'd vows.

Now march the bold confed'rates thro' the plain;
Well hors'd, well clad, a rich and fh'ning train: 30
Meffapus leads the van; and in the rear,
The fons of Tyrrheus in bright arms appear.
In the main battle, with his flaming creft,
The mighty Turnus tow'rs above the reft:
Silent they move; majeftically flow,   35
Like ebbing Nile, or Ganges in his flow.
The Trojans view the dufty cloud from far;
And the dark menace of the diftant war.

Caicus from the rampire faw it rife,
Blackning the fields, and thickning thro' the fkies. 40
Then to his fellows, thus aloud he calls,
What rolling clouds, my friends, approach the walls?
Arm, arm, and man the works; prepare your fpears,
And pointed darts; the Latian hoft appears.
Thus warn'd, theyfhut their gates; with fhouts afcend
The bulwarks, and fecure their foes attend.   46
For their wife gen'ral with forefeeing care,
Had charg'd them not to tempt the doubtful war :
Nor, tho' provok'd, in open fields advance ;
But clofe within their lines attend their chance. 50
Unwilling, yet they keep the ftrict command ;
And fourly wait in arms the hoftile band.
The fiery Turnus flew before the reft,
A pye-ball'd fteed of Thracian ftain he prefs'd ;
His helm of maffy gold ; and crimfon was his creft.
With twenty horfe to fecond his defigns,   56
An unexpected foe, he fac'd the lines.

Is there, he faid, in arms who bravely dare,
His leader's honour, and his danger fhare?
Then fpurring on, his brandifh'd dart he threw, 60
In fign of war; applauding fhouts enfue.

Amaz'd to find a daftard race that run
Behind the rampires, and the battle fhun,

He rides around the camp, with rolling eyes,

And stops at ev'ry post; and ev'ry passage tries.   65

So roams the nightly wolf about the fold,

Wet with descending show'rs, and stiff with cold;

He howls for hunger, and he grins for pain;

His gnashing teeth are exercis'd in vain:

And impotent of anger, finds no way   70

In his distended paws to grasp the prey.

The mothers listen; but the bleating lambs

Securely swig the dug, beneath the dams.

Thus ranges eager Turnus o'er the plain,

Sharp with desire, and furious with disdain: 75

Surveys each passage with a piercing sight;

To force his foes in equal field to fight.

Thus, while he gazes round, at length he spies

Where, fenc'd with strong redoubts, their navy lies;

Close underneath the walls: the washing tide   80

Secures from all approach this weaker side.

He takes the wish'd occasion; fills his hand

With ready fires, and shakes a flaming brand:

Urg'd by his presence, ev'ry soul is warm'd,

And ev'ry hand with kindled firs is arm'd.   85

From the fir'd pines the scatt'ring sparkles fly;

Fat vapours mix'd with flames involve the sky.

What pow'r, O mufes, cou'd avert the flame
Which threaten'd, in the fleet, the Trojan name !
Tell : for the fact, thro' length of time obfcure,   90
Is hard to faith ; yet fhall the fame endure.

   'Tis faid, that when the chief prepar'd his flight,
And fell'd his timber from mount Ida's height,
The grandam goddefs then approach'd her fon,
And with a mother's majefty begun.   95
Grant me, fhe faid, the fole requeft I bring,
Since conquer'd Heav'n has own'd you for its king :
On Ida's brows, for ages paft, there ftood,
With firs and maples fill'd, a fhady wood :
And on the fummit rofe a facred grove,   100
Where I was worfhip'd with religious love ;
Thefe woods, that holy grove, my long delight,
I gave the Trojan prince to fpeed his flight.
Now fill'd with fear, on their behalf I come ;
Let neither winds o'erfet, nor waves intomb   105
The floating forefts of the facred pine ;
But let it be their fafety to be mine.
Then thus reply'd her awful fon ; who rolls
The radiant ftars, and Heav'n and earth controls ;
How dare you, mother, endlefs date demand,   110
For veffels moulded by a mortal hand ?

What then is fate? Shall bold Æneas ride
Of safety certain, on th' uncertain tide?
Yet what I can, I grant: when, wafted o'er,
The chief is landed on the Latian shore,   115
Whatever ships escape the raging storms,
At my command shall change their fading forms
To nymphs divine; and plow the wat'ry way,
Like Dotis and the daughters of the sea.

To seal his sacred vow, by Styx he swore,   120
The lake with liquid pitch, the dreery shore;
And Phlegethon's innavigable flood,
And the black regions of his brother god:
He said; and shook the skies with his imperial nod.

And now at length the number'd hours were come,
Prefix'd by fate's irrevocable doom,   126
When the great mother of the gods was free
To save her ships, and finish Jove's decree.
First, from the quarter of the morn, there sprung
A light that sign'd the heav'ns, and shot along: 130
Then from a cloud, fring'd round with golden fires,
Were timbrels heard, and Berecynthian quires:
And last a voice, with more than mortal sounds,
Both hosts in arms oppos'd, with equal horror wounds.

O Trojan race, your needless aid forbear;   · 135
And know my ships are my peculiar care.

With greater eafe the bold Rutulian may,
With hiffing brands, attempt to burn the fea,
Than finge my facred pines. But you my charge,
Loos'd from your crooked anchors lanch at large, 140
Exalted each a nymph : forfake the fand,
And fwim the feas, at Cybele's command.
No fooner had the goddefs ceas'd to fpeak,
When lo, th' obedient fhips their haulfers break;
And, ftrange to tell, like dolphins in the main, 145
They plunge their prows, and dive, and fpring again:
As many beauteous maids the billows fweep,
As rode before tall veffels on the deep.
The foes furpriz'd with wonder, ftood aghaft,
Meffapus curb'd his fiery courfer's hafte;   150
Old Tiber roar'd; and raifing up his head,
Call'd back his waters to their oozy bed.
Turnus alone, undaunted, bore the fhock;
And with thefe words his trembling troops befpoke.
Thefe monfters for the Trojan's fate are meant, 155
And are by Jove for black prefages fent.
He takes the cowards laft relief away;
For fly they cannot; and, conftrain'd to ftay,
Muft yield unfought, a bafe inglorious prey.
The liquid half of all the globe, is loft;   160
Heav'n fhuts the feas, and we fecure the coaft.

Theirs is no more, than that small spot of ground,
Which myriads of our martial men surround.
Their fates I fear not; or vain oracles;
'Twas giv'n to Venus, they should cross the seas: 165
And land secure upon the Latian plains,
Their promis'd hour is pass'd, and mine remains.
'Tis in the fate of Turnus to destroy
With sword and fire, the faithless race of Troy.
Shall such affronts as these, alone inflame   170
The Grecian brothers, and the Grecian name?
My cause and theirs is one; a fatal strife,
And final ruin, for a ravish'd wife.
Was't not enough, that punish'd for the crime,
They fell; but will they fall a second time?   175
One wou'd have thought they paid enough before,
To curse the costly sex; and durst offend no more.
Can they securely trust their feeble wall,
A slight partition, a thin interval,
Betwixt their fate and them; when Troy, tho' built
By hands divine, yet perish'd by their guilt?   181
Lend me, for once, my friends, your valiant hands,
To force from out their lines these dastard bands.
Less than a thousand ships will end this war;
Nor Vulcan needs his fated arms prepare.   185

Let all the Tuſcans, all th' Arcadians join,
Nor theſe, nor thoſe ſhall fruſtrate my deſign.
Let them not fear the treaſons of the night;
The robb'd palladium, the pretended flight:
Our onſet ſhall be made in open light.   190
No wooden engine ſhall their town betray,
Fires they ſhall have around, but fires by day.
No Grecian babes before their camp appear,
Whom Hector's arms detain'd, to the tenth tardy year.
Now, ſince the ſun is rolling to the weſt,   195
Give me the ſilent night to needful reſt:
Refreſh your bodies, and your arms prepare,
The morn ſhall end the ſmall remains of war.

  The poſt of honour to Meſſapus falls,
To keep the nightly guard; to watch the walls; 200
To pitch the fires at diſtances around,
And cloſe the Trojans in their ſcanty ground.
Twice ſeven Rutulian captains ready ſtand:
And twice ſeven hundred horſe their chiefs command:
All clad in ſhining arms the works inveſt;   205
Each with a radiant helm, and waving creſt.
Stretch'd at their length, they preſs the graſſy ground;
They laugh, they ſing, the jolly bowls go round:
With lights, and chearful fires renew the day;
And paſs the wakeful night in feaſts and play.   210

The Trojans, from above, their foes beheld;
And with arm'd legions all the rampires fill'd:
Seiz'd with affright, their gates they first explore;
Join works to works with bridges; tow'r to tow'r:
Thus all things needful for defence abound;   215
Mneftheus, and brave Serefthus walk the round:
Commiffion'd by their abfent prince, to fhare
The common danger, and divide the care.
The foldiers draw their lots; and as they fall,
By turns relieve each other on the wall.   220

Nigh where the foes their utmoft guards advance
To watch the gate, was warlike Nifus chance.
His father Hyrtacus of noble blood;
His mother was a hunt'refs of the wood:
And fent him to the wars; well cou'd he bear   225
His lance in fight, and dart the flying fpear:
But better fkill'd unerring fhafts to fend:
Befide him ftood Euryalus his friend.
Euryalus, than whom the Trojan hoft
No fairer face, or fweeter air could boaft.   230
Scare had the down to fhade his cheeks begun;
One was their care, and their delight was one.
One common hazard in the war they fhar'd;
And now were both by choice upon the guard.

Then Nisus, thus: Or do the gods inspire　235.
This warmth, or make we gods of our desire?
A gen'rous ardour boils within my breast,
Eager of action, enemy to rest:
This urges me to fight, and fires my mind,
To leave a memorable name behind.　　　240
Thou seest the foe secure: how faintly shine
Their scatter'd fires! the most in sleep supine
Along the ground, an easy conquest lie;
The wakeful few, the fuming flaggon ply:
All hush around.　Now hear what I revolve;　245.
A thought unripe, and scarcely yet resolve.
Our absent prince both camp and council mourn;
By message both wou'd hasten his return:
If they confer what I demand, on thee,
(For fame is recompence enough for me)　　250.
Methinks, beneath yon hill, I have espy'd
A way that safely will my passage guide.
Euryalus stood list'ning while he spoke;
With love of praise, and noble envy struck;
Then to his ardent friend expos'd his mind:　255
All this alone, and leaving me behind,
Am I unworthy, Nisus, to be join'd?
Think'st thou I can my share of glory yield,
Or send thee unassisted to the field;

Not fo my father taught my childhood arms,   260
Born in a fiege, and bred among alarms ;
Nor is my youth unworthy of my friend,
Nor of the heav'n-born hero I attend.
The thing call'd life, with eafe I can difclaim ;
And think it over-fold to purchafe fame.   265

Then Nifus, thus : Alas ! thy tender years
Wou'd minifter new matter to my fears :
So may the gods, who view this friendly ftrife,
Reftore me to thy lov'd embrace with life,
Condemn'd to pay my vows (as fure I truft)   270
This thy requeft is cruel and unjuft.
But if fome chance, as many chances are,
And doubtful hazards in the deeds of war ;
If one fhould reach my head, there let it fall,
And fpare thy life ; I wou'd not perifh all.   275
Thy bloomy youth deferves a longer date ;
Live thou to mourn thy love's unhappy fate :
To bear my mangled body from the foe ;
Or buy it back, and fun'ral rites beftow.
Or if hard fortune fhall thofe dues deny,   280
Thou canft at leaft an empty tomb fupply.
O let not me the widow's tears renew ;
Nor let a mother's curfe my name purfue ;

Thy pious parent, who for love of thee,
Forfook the coafts of friendly Sicily,   285
Her age, committing to the feas and wind,
When ev'ry weary matron ftaid behind.
To this Euryalus : You plead in vain,
And but protract the caufe you cannot gain :
No more delays, but hafte. With that he wakes 290
The nodding watch ; each to his office takes.
The guard reliev'd, the gen'rous couple went
To find the council at the royal tent.
All creatures elfe forgot their daily care ;
And fleep, the common gift of nature, fhare :   295
Except the Trojan peers, who wakeful fate
In nightly council for th' endanger'd ftate.
They vote a meffage to their abfent chief ;
Shew their diftrefs ; and beg a fwift relief.
Amid the camp a filent feat they chofe,   300
Remote from clamour, and fecure from foes.
On their left arms their ample fhields they bear,
Their right reclin'd upon the bending fpear.
Now Nifus and his friend approach the guard,
And beg admiffion, eager to be heard :   305
Th' affair important, not to be deferr'd.
Afcanius bids 'em be conducted in ;
Ord'ring the more experienc'd to begin.

Then Nifus thus.   Ye fathers, lend your ears,
Nor judge our bold attempt beyond our years.   310
The foe fecurely drench'd in fleep and wine,
Neglect their watch; the fires but thinly fhine:
And where the fmoke, in cloudy vapours flies,
Cov'ring the plain, and curling to the fkies,
Betwixt two paths, which at the gate divide,   315 ⎫
Clofe by the fea, a paffage we have fpy'd,   ⎬
Which will our way to great Æneas guide.   ⎭
Expect each hour to fee him fafe again,
Loaded with fpoils of foes in battle flain.
Snatch we the lucky minute while we may: 320
Nor can we be miftaken in the way;
For hunting in the vales we both have feen
The rifing turrets, and the ftream between:
And know the winding courfe, with ev'ry ford.
He ceas'd: and old Alethes took the word.   325
Our country gods, in whom our truft we place,
Will yet from ruin fave the Trojan race:
While we behold fuch dauntlefs worth appear
In dawning youth; and fouls fo void of fear.
Then, into tears of joy the father broke;   330 ⎫
Each in his longing arms by turns he took: ⎬
Panted and paus'd; and thus again he fpoke.   ⎭

Ye brave young men, what equal gifts can we,
In recompence of fuch defert, decree?
The greateft, fure, and beft you can receive,   335
The gods, and your own confcious worth will give.
The reft our grateful gen'ral will beftow;
And young Afcanius till his manhood owe.

And I, whofe welfare in my father lies,
Afcanius adds, by the great deities,   340
By my dear country, by my houfhold-gods,
By hoary Vefta's rites, and dark abodes,
Adjure you both; (on you my fortune ftands,
That and my faith I plight into your hands:)
Make me but happy in his fafe return,   345
Whofe wanted prefence I can only mourn;
Your common gift fhall two large goblets be
Of filver, wrought with curious imagery;
And high embofs'd, which, when old Priam reign'd,
My conqu'ring fire at fack'd Arifba gain'd.   350
And more, two tripods caft in antick mould,
With two great talents of the fineft gold:
Befide a coftly bowl, ingrav'd with art,
Which Dido gave, when firft fhe gave her heart.
But if in conquer'd Italy we reign,   355
When fpoils by lot the victor fhall obtain,

Thou faw'ft the courfer by proud Turnus prefs'd,
That, Nifus, and his arms, and nodding creft,
And fhield, from chance exempt, fhall be thy fhare;
Twelve lab'ring flaves, twelve handmaids young
                                    [and fair,
And clad in rich attire, and train'd with care.
And laft, a Latian field with fruitful plains,
And a large portion of the king's domains.
But thou, whofe years are more to mine ally'd,
No faté my vow'd affeſtion fhall divide   365
From thee, heroick youth; be wholly mine:
Take full poffeffion; all my foul is thine.
One faith, one fame, one fate fhall both attend;
My life's companion, and my bofom friend;
My peace fhall be committed to thy care,   370
And to thy conduſt, my concerns in war.

   Then thus the young Euryalus reply'd;
Whatever fortune, good or bad betide,
The fame fhall be my age, as now my youth;
No time fhall find me wanting to my truth.   375
This only from your goodnefs let me gain;
(And this ungranted, all rewards are vain)
Of Priam's royal race my mother came;
And fure the beft that ever bore the name:

J. Collyer sculp.

Whom neither Troy, nor Sicily cou'd hold   380
From me departing, but o'erspent, and old,
My fate she follow'd; ignorant of this,
Whatever danger, neither parting kiss,
Nor pious blessing taken, her I leave;
And, in this only act of all my life deceive.   385
By this right hand, and conscious night I swear,
My soul so sad a farewel could not bear.
Be you her comfort; fill my vacant place,
(Permit me to presume so great a grace)
Support her age, forsaken and distress'd;   390
That hope alone will fortify my breast
Against the worst of fortunes, and of fears.
He said: The mov'd assistants melt in tears.
Then thus Ascanius, wonder-struck to see
That image of his filial piety;   395
So great beginnings, in so green an age,
Exact the faith, which 1 again engage.
Thy mother all the dues shall justly claim
Creüsa had; and only want the name.
Whate'er event thy bold attempt shall have,   400
'Tis merit to have born a son so brave.
Now by my head, a sacred oath, I swear,
(My father us'd it) what returning here

Crown'd with fuccefs, I for thyfelf prepare,
That, if thou fail, fhall thy lov'd mother fhare. 405

He faid; and weeping while he fpoke the word,
From his broad belt he drew a fhining fword,
Magnificent with gold. Lycaon made,
And in an iv'ry fcabbard fheath'd the blade:
This was his gift: greatMneftheus gave his friend410
A lion's hide, his body to defend:
And good Alethes furnifh'd him befide,
With his own trufty helm, of temper try'd.

Thus arm'd they went. The noble Trojans wait
Their iffuing forth, and follow to the gate. 415
With prayers and vows, above the reft appears
Afcanius, manly far beyond his years.
And meffages committed to their care.
Which all in winds were loft, and flitting air.

The trenches firft they pafs'd; then took their way
Where their proud foes in pitch'd pavilions lay; 421
To many fatal, ere themfelves were flain:
They found the carelefs hoft difpers'd upon the plain.
Who gorg'd, and drunk with wine, fupinely fnore:
Unharnefs'd chariots ftand along the fhore: 425
Amidft the wheels and reins, the goblet by,
A medly of debauch and war they lie.

erving Nifus fhew'd his friend the fight;
old a conqueft gain'd without a fight.
afion offers, and I ftand prepar'd: 430
ere lies our way; be thou upon the guard,
I look around; while I fecurely go,
d hew a paffage, thro' the fleeping foe.
tly he fpoke; then ftriding, took his way,
ith his drawn fword, where haughty Rhamnes lay:
s head rais'd high, on tapeftry beneath, 436
id heaving from his breaft, he drew his breath:
king and prophet by king Turnus lov'd;
it fate by prefcience cannot be remov'd,
im, and his fleeping flaves he flew. Then fpies 440
here Rhemus, with his rich retinue lies:
is armour-bearer firft, and next he kills
is charioteer, intrench'd betwixt the wheels
nd his lov'd horfes: laft invades their lord;
ull on his neck he drives the fatal fword: 445
he gafping head flies off; a purple flood
lows from the trunk, that welters in the blood:
Vhich by the fpurning heels, difpers'd around,
The bed befprinkles, and bedews the ground.
amus the bold, and Lamyrus the ftrong, 450
le flew; and then Serranus fair and young.

From dice and wine the youth retir'd to reft,
And puff'd the fumy god from out his breaft:
Ev'n then he dreamt of drink and lucky play;
More lucky had it lafted 'till the day.　　455

　　The famifh'd lion thus, with hunger bold,
O'erleaps the fences of the nightly fold;
And tears the peaceful flocks: with filent awe
Trembling they lie, and pant beneath his paw.

　　Nor with lefs rage Euryalus employs　　460
The wrathful fword, or fewer foes deftroys:
But on th' ignoble crowd his fury flew:
He Fadus, Hebefus, and Rhætus flew.
Opprefs'd with heavy fleep the former fall,
But Rhætus wakeful, and obferving all,　　465
Behind a fpacious jar he flink'd for fear:
The fatal iron found, and reach'd him there.
For as he rofe, it pierc'd his naked fide,
And reeking, thence return'd in crimfon dy'd.
The wound pours out a ftream of wine and blood,
The purple foul comes floating in the flood.　　471

　　Now where Meffapus quarter'd they arrive;
The fires were fainting there, and juft alive.
The warrior-horfes ty'd in order fed;
Nifus obferv'd the difcipline, and faid,　　475

ur eager thirſt of blood may both betray;
nd ſee the ſcatter'd ſtreaks of dawning day,
oe to noƈturnal thefts: No more, my friend,
Iere let our glutted execution end:
A lane through ſlaughter'd bodies we have made: 480
The bold Euryalus, tho' loth, obey'd.
Of arms, and arras, and of plate they find
A precious load; but theſe they leave behind.
Yet fond of gaudy ſpoils the boy would ſtay
To make the rich capariſon his prey,   485
Which on the ſteed of conquer'd Rhamnes lay.
Nor did his eyes leſs longingly behold
The girdle belt, with nails of burniſh'd gold.
This preſent Cedicus the rich, beſtow'd
On Remulus, when friendſhip firſt they vow'd: 490
And abſent, join'd in hoſpitable tyes;
He dying, to his heir bequeath'd the prize:
Till by the conqu'ring Ardean troops oppreſs'd
He fell; and they the glorious gift poſſeſs'd.
Theſe glitt'ring ſpoils (now made the victor's gain)
He to his body ſuits; but ſuits in vain.   496
Meſſapus' helm he finds among the reſt,
And laces on, and wears the waving creſt.
Proud of their conqueſt, prouder of their prey,
They leave the camp; and take the ready way. 500

But far they had not pafs'd, before they fpy'd
Three hundred horfe with Volfcens for their guide.
The queen a legion to king Turnus fent,
But the fwift horfe the flower foot prevent:
And now advancing fought the leader's tent. 505
They faw the pair; for thro' the doubtful fhade
His fhining helm Euryalus betray'd,
On which the moon with full reflexion play'd.
'Tis not for nought, cry'd Volfcens, from the crowd,
Thefe men go there; then rais'd his voice aloud: 510
Stand, ftand: why thus in arms, and whither bent:
From whence, to whom, and on what errand fent?
Silent they fcud away, and hafte their flight,
To neighbouring woods, and truftthemfelvestonight.
The fpeedy horfe all paffages belay. 515
And fpur their fmoking fteeds to crofs their way;
And watch each entrance of the winding wood;
Black was the foreft, thick with beach it ftood;
Horrid with fern, and intricate with thorn,
Few paths of human feet or tracks of beaftswereworn.
The darknefs of the fhades, his heavy prey, 521
And fear, mif-led the younger from his way.
But Nifus hit the turns with happier hafte,
And thoughtlefs of his friend, the foreft pafs'd:

And Alban plains, from Alba's name fo call'd, 525
Where king Latinus then his oxen ftall'd.
Till turning at the length, he ftood his ground,
And mifs'd his friend, and caft his eyes around;
Ah wretch, he cry'd, where have I left behind
Th' unhappy youth, where fhall I hope to find? 530
Or what way take I   Again he ventures back:
And treads the mazes of his former track.
He winds the wood, and lift'ning hears the noife
Of trampling courfers, and the riders voice.
The found approach'd, and fuddenly he view'd 535
The foes inclofing, and his friend purfu'd:
Forelay'd and taken, while he ftrove in vain,
The fhelter of the friendly fhades to gain.
What fhou'd he next attempt! what arms employ,
What fruitlefs force to free the captive boy? 540
Or defperate fhould he rufh and lofe his life,
With odds opprefs, in fuch unequal ftrife?
Refolv'd at length, his pointed fpear he fhook;
And cafting on the moon a mournful look,
Guardian of groves, and goddefs of the night, 545
Fair queen, he faid, direct my dart aright:
If e'er my pious father for my fake
Did grateful off'rings on thy altars make;

Or I increas'd them with my sylvan toils,
And hung thy holy roofs, with savage spoils;   550
Give me to scatter these.   Then from his ear
He pois'd, and aim'd, and lanch'd the trembling spear.
The deadly weapon, hissing from the grove,
Impetuous on the back of Sulmo drove;
Pierc'd his thin armour, drank his vital blood,   555
And in his body left the broken wood.
He staggers round, his eyeballs roll in death,
And with short sobs he gasps away his breath.
All stand amaz'd; a second jav'lin flies,
With equal strength, and quivers thro' the skies;   560
This thro' thy temples, Tagus, forc'd the way,
And in the brain-pan warmly bury'd lay.
Fierce Volscens foams with rage, and gazing round,
Descry'd not him who gave the fatal wound:
Nor knew to fix revenge: but thou, he cries,   565
Shall pay for both, and at the pris'ner flies
With his drawn sword. Then struck with deep despair,
That cruel sight the lover cou'd not bear:
But from his covert rush'd in open view,
And sent his voice before him as he flew.   570
Me, me, he cry'd, turn all your swords alone
On me; the fact confess'd, the fault my own.

He neither cou'd nor durſt, the guiltleſs youth;
Ye moon and ſtars bear witneſs to the truth !
His only crime, (if friendſhip can offend)   575
Is too much love to his unhappy friend.
Too late he ſpeaks; the ſword, which fury guides,
Driv'n with full force, had pierc'd his tender ſides.
Down fell the beauteous youth; the yawning wound
Guſh'd out a purple ſtream, and ſtain'd the ground.
His ſnowy neck reclines upon his breaſt,   581
Like a fair flow'r by the keen ſhare oppreſs'd :
Like a white poppy ſinking on the plain,
Whoſe heavy head is overcharg'd with rain.
Deſpair, and rage, and vengeance juſtly vow'd, 585
Drove Niſus headlong on the hoſtile crowd :
Volſcens he ſeeks; on him alone he bends :
Born back, and bor'd, by his ſurrounding friends,
Onward he preſs'd : and kept him ſtill in ſight;
Then whirl'd aloft his ſword, with all his might: 590
Th' unerring ſteel deſcended while he ſpoke;
Pierc'd his wide mouth, and thro' his weazon broke:
Dying he flew; and ſtagg'ring on the plain,
With ſwimming eyes he ſought his lover ſlain :
Then quiet on his bleeding boſom fell;   595
Content in death, to be reveng'd ſo well.

C 2

O happy friends! for if my verſe can give
Immortal life, your fame ſhall ever live:
Fix'd as the capitol's foundation lies;
And ſpread, where e'er the Roman eagle flies!   600

    The conqu'ring party firſt divide the prey,
Then their ſlain leader to the camp convey.
With wonder, as they went, the troops were fill'd,
To ſee ſuch numbers whom ſo few had kill'd.
Serranus, Rhamnes, and the reſt they found;   605 ⎫
Vaſt crowds the dying and the dead ſurround: ⎬
And the yet reeking blood o'erflows the ground.   ⎭
All knew the helmet which Meſſapus loſt;
But mourn'd a purchaſe that ſo dear had coſt.
Now roſe the ruddy morn from Tithon's bed;   610
And with the dawn of day, the ſkies o'erſpread.
Nor long the ſun his daily courſe withheld,
But added colours to the world reveal'd.
When early Turnus wak'ning with the light,
All clad in armour calls his troops to fight.   615
His martial men with fierce harangues he fir'd;
And his own ardor, in their ſouls inſpir'd.
This done, to give new terror to his foes,
The heads of Niſus, and his friend he ſhows,
Rais'd high on pointed ſpears: A ghaſtly ſight; 620
Loud peals of ſhouts enſue, and barbarous delight.

. Mean time the Trojans run, where danger calls,
They line their trenches, and they man their walls:
In front extended to the left they stood :
Safe was the right surrounded by the flood.   625
But casting from their tow'rs a frightful view,
They saw the faces, which too well they knew;
Tho' then disguis'd in death, and smear'd all o'er .
With filth obscene, and dropping putrid gore.
Soon hasty fame, thro' the sad city bears   630
The mournful message to the mother's ears :
An icy cold benumbs her limbs: she shakes :
Her cheeks the blood, her hand the web forsakes.
She runs the rampires round amidst the war,
Nor fears the flying darts : she rends her hair, 635
And fills with loud laments the liquid air.
Thus then, my lov'd Euryalus appears ;
Thus looks the prop of my declining years !
Was't on this face, my famish'd eyes I fed !
Ah how unlike the living, is the dead !   640
And could'st thou leave me, cruel, thus alone,
Not one kind kiss from a departing son !
No look, no last adieu before he went,
In an ill-boding hour to slaughter sent !

C 3

Cold on the ground, and preffing foreign clay,   645
To Latian dogs, and fowls he lies a prey !
Nor was I near to clofe his dying eyes,
To wafh his wounds, to weep his obfequies :
To call about his corps his crying friends,
Or fpread the mantle, (made for other ends,)   650
On his dear body, which I wove with care,
Nor did my daily pains, or nightly labour fpare.
Where fhall I find his corps, what earth fuftains
His trunk difmember'd, and his cold remains ?
For this, alas, I left my needful eafe,   655
Expos'd my life to winds, and winter feas !
If any pity touch Rutulian hearts,
Here empty all your quivers, all your darts :
Or if they fail, thou Jove conclude my woe,
And fend me thunder-ftruck to fhades below !   660
      Her fhrieks and clamours pierce the Trojans ears,
Unman their courage, and augment their fears :
Nor young Afcanius cou'd the fight fuftain,
Nor old Ilioneus his tears reftrain :
But Actor and Idæus, jointly fent,   665.
To bear the madding mother to her tent.
And now the trumpets terribly from far,
With rattling clangor, rouze the fleepy war.

The foldiers fhouts fucceed the brazen founds,
And heav'n, from pole to pole, their noife rebounds.
The Volfcians bear their fhields upon their head, 671
And rufhing forward, form a moving fhed ;
Thefe fill the ditch, thofe pull the bulwarks down :
Some raife the ladders, others fcale the town.
But where void fpaces on the walls appear,   675
Or thin defence, they pour their forces there.
With poles and miffive weapons, from afar,
The Trojans keep aloof the rifing war.
Taught by their ten years fiege defenfive fight ;
They roll down ribs of rocks, and unrefifted weight:
To break the penthoufe with the pond'rous blow ; 681
Which yet the patient Volfcians undergo.
But cou'd not bear th' unequal combat long ;
For where the Trojans find the thickeft throng,
The ruin falls : their fhatter'd fhields give way, 685
And their crufh'd heads become an eafy prey.
They fhrink for fear, abated of their rage,
No longer dare in a blind fight engage.
Contented now to gall them from below
With darts and flings, and with the diftant bow. 690
   Elfewhere Mezentius, terrible to view,
A blazing pine within the trenches threw.

But brave Meſſapus, Neptune's warlike ſon,
Broke down the palifades, the trenches won,
And loud for ladders calls, to ſcale the town. 695

 Calliope begin : ye ſacred nine,
Inſpire your poet in his high deſign :
To ſing what ſlaughter manly Turnus made :
What ſouls he ſent below the Stygian ſhade.
What fame the ſoldiers with their captain ſhare, 700
And the vaſt circuit of the fatal war.
For you in ſinging martial facts excel ;
You beſt remember ; and alone can tell.

 There ſtood a tow'r, amazing to the ſight,
Built up of beams ; and of ſtupendous height ; 705
Art, and the nature of the place conſpir'd
To furniſh all the ſtrength that war requir'd.
To level this, the bold Italians join ;
The wary Trojans obviate their deſign : 709
With weighty ſtones o'erwhelm'd their troops below,
Shoot thro' the Loopholes, and ſharp jav'lins throw.
Turnus, the chief, toſs'd from his thund'ring hand,
Againſt the wooden walls, a flaming brand :
It ſtuck, the fiery plague : the winds were high ;
The planks were ſeaſon'd, and the timber dry. 715
Contagion caught the poſts : it ſpread along,
Scorch'd, and to diſtance drove the ſcatter'd throng.

The Trojans fled; the fire purfu'd amain,
Still gathering faft upon the trembling train;
Till crowding to the corners of the wall,   720
Down the defence, and the defenders fall.
The mighty flaw makes heav'n itfelf refound,
The dead, and dying Trojans ftrew the ground.
The tow'r that follow'd on the fallen crew,   724
Whelm'd o'er their heads, and bury'd whom it flew:
Some ftuck upon the darts themfelves had fent;
All, the fame equal ruin underwent.

Young Lycus and Helenor only fcape;
Sav'd how they know not, from the fteepy leap:
Helenor, elder of the two; by birth,   730
On one fide royal, one a fon of earth,
Whom to the Lydian king, Lycimnia bare,
And fent her boafted baftard to the war:
'A privilege which none but freemen fhare.)
Slight were his arms, a fword and filver fhield,   735
No marks of honour charg'd its empty field.
Light as he fell, fo light the youth arofe,
And rifing, found himfelf amidft his foes.
Nor flight was left, nor hopes to force his way;
Embolden'd by defpair, he ftood at bay;   740
C 5

And like a ftag, whom all the troop furrounds
Of eager huntfmen, and invading hounds ;
Refolv'd on death, he diffipates his fears,
And bounds aloft, againft the pointed fpears :
So dares the youth, fecure of death ; and throws 745
His dying body, on his thickeft foes.

    But Lycus, fwifter of his feet, by far,
Runs, doubles, winds and turns, amidft the war :
Springs to the walls, and leaves his foes behind,
And fnatches at the beam he firft can find.   750
Looks up, and leaps aloft at all the ftretch,
In hopes the helping hand of fome kind friend to reach,.
But Turnus follow'd hard his hunted prey,.
(His fpear had almoft reach'd him in the way,
Short of his reins, and fcare a fpan behind,)   755.
Fool, faid the chief, tho' fleeter than the wind,
Coud'ft thou prefume to fcape, when I purfue ?
He faid, and downward by the feet he drew
The trembling daftard : at the tug he falls,.
Vaft ruins come along, rent from the fmoking walls.
Thus on fome filver fwan, or tim'rous hare,   761
Jove's bird comes fowfing down, from upper air ;
Her crooked talons trufs the fearful fray :
Then out of fight fhe foars, and wings her way.

So feizes the grim wolf the tender lamb,   765
In vain lamented by the bleating dam.

  Then rufhing onward, with a barb'rous cry,
The troops of Turnus to the combat fly.
The ditch with faggots fill'd, the daring foe
Tofs'd firebrands to the fteepy turrets throw.   770

   Hilioneus, as bold Lucetius came
To force the gate, and feed the kindling flame,
Roll'd down the fragment of a rock fo right,
It crufh'd him double underneath the weight.
Two more young Liger and Afylas flew ;   775 }
To bend the bow young Liger better knew :
Afylas beft the pointed jav'lin threw.
Brave Cæneas laid Ortygius on the plain,
The victor Cæneas was by Turnus flain.
By the fame hand, Clonis and Itys fall;   780
Sagar and Ida, ftanding on the wall.
From Capy's arms his fate Privernus found ;
Hurt by Themilla firft ; but flight the wound ;
His fhield thrown by, to mitigate the fmart,
He clapt his hand upon the wounded part :   785
The fecond fhaft came fwift and unefpy'd,
And pierc'd his hand, and nail'd it to his fide :

Transfix'd his breathing lungs, and beating heart;
The soul came issuing out, and hiss'd against the dart.

    The son of Arcens shone amid the rest,   790
In glitt'ring armour and a purple vest.
Fair was his face, his eyes inspiring love,
Bred by his father in the Martian grove:
Where the fat altars of Palicus flame,
And sent in arms to purchase early fame.   795
Him, when he spy'd from far the Thuscan king,
Laid by the lance and took him to the sling:
Thrice whirl'd the thong around his head, and threw:
The heated lead half melted as it flew:
It pierc'd his hollow temples and his brain: 800
The youth came tumbling down, and spurn'd the plain.

    Then young Ascanius, who before this day
Was wont in woods to shoot the savage prey,
First bent in martial strife, the twanging bow;
And exercis'd against a human foe.   805
With this bereft Numanus of his life,
Who Turnus' younger sister took to wife.
Proud of his realm, and of his royal bride,
Vaunting before his troops, and lengthen'd with
                [a stride,
In these insulting terms the Trojans he defy'd. 810

Twice conquer'd cowards, now your shame is shown,
Coop'd up a second time within your town !
Who dare not issue forth in open field,
But hold your walls before you for a shield.
Thus threat you war, thus our alliance force !   815
What gods, what madness hither steer'd your course !
You shall not find the sons of Atreus here,
Nor need the frauds of sly Ulysses fear.
Strong from the cradle, of a sturdy brood,
We bear our new-born infants to the flood ;   820
There bath'd amid the stream, our boys we hold,
With winter harden'd, and inur'd to cold.
They wake before the day to range the wood,
Kill ere they eat, nor taste unconquer'd food.
No sports, but what belong to war they know,   825
To break the stubborn colt, to bend the bow.
Our youth, of labour patient, earn their bread ;
Hardly they work, with frugal diet fed.
From ploughs and harrows sent to seek renown,
They fight in fields, and storm the shaken town. 830
No part of life from toils of war is free ;
No change in age, or diff'rence in degree.
We plough, and til in arms ; our oxen feel,
Instead of goads, the spur, and pointed steel :

Th' inverted lance makes furrows in the plain; 835
Ev'n time that changes all, yet changes us in vain: .
The body, not the mind : nor can control
Th' immortal vigour, or abate the soul.
Our helms defend the young, disguise the grey :
We live by plunder, and delight in prey.   840
Your vests embroider'd with rich purple shine :
In sloth you glory, and in dances join.
Your vests have sweeping sleeves : with female pride,
Your turbants underneath your chins are ty'd.
Go Phrygians, to your Dindymus agen;   845
Go, less than women, in the shapes of men.
Go, mix'd with eunuchs, in the mother's rites,
Where with unequal sound the flute invites.
Sing, dance, and howl by turns in Ida's shade;
Resign the war to men, who know the martial trade.

    This foul reproach, Ascanius cou'd not hear 851
With patience, or a vow'd revenge forbear.
At the full stretch of both his hands, he drew,
And almost join'd the horns of the tough eugh.
But first, before the throne of Jove he stood :   855
And thus with lifted hands invok'd the god.
My first attempt, great Jupiter, succeed ;
An annual off'ring in thy grove shall bleed :

A fnow-white fteer, before thy altar led,
Who like his mother bears aloft his head,   860
Butswith histhreat'ning brows,and bellowingftands,
And dares the fight, and fpurns the yellow fands.

   Jove bow'd the heav'ns, and lent a gracious ear,
And thunder'd on the left, amidft the clear.
Sounded at once the bow; and fwiftly flies   865
The feather'd death, and hiffes thro' the fkies.
The fteel thro' both his temples forc'd the way:
Extended on the ground Numanus lay.
Go now, vain boafter, and true valour fcorn; · 869
The Phrygians, twice fubdu'd, yet make this third·

                              [return.

Afcanius faid no more: the Trojans fhake·
The heav'ns with fhouting, and new vigour take.

   Apollo then beftrode a golden cloud,
To view the feats of arms, and fighting crowd;
And thus the beardlefs victor, he befpoke aloud. 875
Advance illuftrious youth, increafe in fame,
And wide from eaft to weft extend thy name.
Offspring of gods thyfelf; and Rome fhall owe
To thee, a race of demigods below.
This is the way to heav'n: the pow'rs divine , 880
From this beginning date the Julian line.

To thee, to them, and their victorious heirs,

The conquer'd war is due: and the vaſt world is theirs.

Troy is too narrow for thy name.   He ſaid,

And plunging downward ſhot his radiant head; 885

Diſpell'd the breathing air, that broke his flight,

Shorn of his beams, a man to mortal ſight.

Old Butes' form he took, Anchiſes' ſquire,

Now left to rule Aſcanius, by his ſire;

His wrinkled viſage, and his hoary hairs,   890⎤

His mien, his habit, and his arms he wears;   ⎬

And thus ſalutes the boy, too forward for his years.⎦

Suffice it thee, thy father's worthy ſon,

The warlike prize thou haſt already won :

The god of archers gives thy youth a part   895

Of his own praiſe; nor envies equal art.

Now tempt the war no more.   He ſaid, and flew

Obſcure in air, and vaniſh'd from their view.

The Trojans, by his arms, their patron know;

And hear the twanging of his heav'nly bow. 900

Then duteous force they uſe, and Phœbus' name,

To keep from fight the youth too fond of fame.

Undaunted they themſelves no danger ſhun :

From wall to wall, the ſhouts and clamours run:

Theybend their bows, theywhirltheirflings around:
Ieaps of spent arrows fall, and strew the ground;
And helms, and shields, and rattling arms resound.
The combat thickens, like the storm that flies
From westward, when the show'ry kids arise:
Or patt'ring hail comes pouring on the main,   910
When Jupiter descends in harden'd rain.
Or bellowing clouds burst with a stormy sound,
And with an armed winter strew the ground.

  Pand'rus and Bitias, thunder-bolts of war,
Whom Hiera to bold Alcanor bare   915
On Ida's top, two youths of height and size,
Like firs that on their mother-mountain rise:
Presuming on their force, the gates unbar,
And of their own accord invite the war.
With fates averse, against their king's command, 920
Arm'd on the right, and on the left they stand,
And flank the passage: shining steel they wear,
And waving crests above their heads appear.
Thus two tall oaks, that Padus' banks adorn,
Lift up to heav'n their leafy heads unshorn;   925
And overpress'd with nature's heavy load,
Dance to the whistling winds, and at each other nod:
In flows a tide of Latians, when they see
The gate set open, and the passage free.

Bold Quercens, with rash Tmarus rushing on, 930
Equicolus, that in bright armour shone,
And Hæmon first, but soon repuls'd they fly,
Or in the well-defended pass they die.
These with success are fir'd, and those with rage;
And each on equal terms at length engage.   935
Drawn from their lines, and issuing on the plain,
The Trojans hand to hand the fight maintain.

    Fierce Turnus in another quarter fought,
When suddenly th' unhop'd-for news was brought;
The foes had left the fastness of their place,   940
Prevail'd in fight, and had his men in chace.
He quits th' attack, and, to prevent their fate,
Runs, where the giant brothers guard the gate.
The first he met, Antiphates the brave,
But base begotten on a Theban slave;   945
Sarpedon's son he slew: the deadly dart
Found passage thro' his breast, and pierc'd his heart.
Fix'd in the wound th' Italian cornel stood;
Warm'd in his lungs, and in his vital blood.
Aphidnus next, and Erymanthus dies,   950
And Meropes, and the gigantick size
Of Bitias, threat'ning with his ardent eyes.
Not by the feeble dart he fell oppress'd,
A dart were lost within that roomy breast;

3ut from a knotted lance, large, heavy, ſtrong; 955
Which roar'd like thunder as it whirl'd along:
Not two bull-hides th' impetuous force withhold;
Nor coat of double mail, with ſcales of gold.
Down ſunk the monſter bulk, and preſs'd the ground:
His arms and clatt'ring ſhield, on the vaſt body ſound.
Not with leſs ruin, than the Bajan mole,   961
(Rais'd on the ſeas the ſurges to control,)
At once comes tumbling down the rocky wall,
Prone to the deep the ſtones disjointed fall
Off the vaſt pile; the ſcatter'd ocean flies;   965
Black ſands, diſcolour'd froth, and mingled mud ariſe.
The frighted billows roll, and ſeek the ſhores:
Then trembles Prochyta, then Iſchia roars:
Typhœus thrown beneath, by Jove's command,
Aſtoniſh'd at the flaw, that ſhakes the land.   970
Soon ſhifts his weary ſide, and ſcarce awake,
With wonder feels the weight preſs lighter on his back.
   The warrior-god the Latian troops inſpir'd;
New ſtrung their ſinews, and their courage fir'd,
But chills the Trojan hearts with cold affright: 975
Then black deſpair precipitates their flight.
   When Pandarus beheld his brother kill'd,
The town with fear, and wild confuſion fill'd,

He turns the hinges of the heavy gate 979
With both his hands; and adds his ſhoulders to the
[weight.
Some happier friends within the walls incloſ'd;
The reſt ſhut out, to certain death expoſ'd.
Fool as he was, and frantick in his care,
T' admit young Turnus, and include the war.
He thruſt amid the crowd, ſecurely bold; 985
Like a fierce tiger pent amid the fold.
Too late his blazing buckler they deſcry;
And ſparkling fires that ſhot from either eye:
His mighty members, and his ample breaſt,
His rattling armour, and his crimſon creſt. 990
 Far from that hated face the Trojans fly;
All but the fool who ſought his deſtiny.
Mad Pandarus ſteps forth, with vengeance vow'd
For Bitias' death, and threatens thus aloud.
Theſe are not Ardea's walls, nor this the town 995
Amata proffers with Lavinia's crown:
'Tis hoſtile earth you tread; of hope bereft,
No means of ſafe return by flight are left.
To whom with count'nance calm, and ſoul ſedate,
Thus Turnus: Then begin; and try thy fate: 1000
My meſſage to the ghoſt of Priam bear,
Tell him a new Achilles ſent thee there.

A lance of tough ground-ash the Trojan threw,
ough in the rind, and knotted as it grew,
/ith his full force he whirl'd it first around; 1005
ut the soft yielding air receiv'd the wound:
nperial Juno turn'd the course before;
nd fix'd the wand'ring weapon in the door.

But hope not thou, said Turnus, when I strike,
'o shun thy fate, our force is not alike: 1010
[or thy steel temper'd by the Lemnian god:
'hen rising, on his utmost stretch he stood:
ind aim'd from high: the full descending blow
]leaves the broad front, and beardless cheeks in two:
)own sinks the giant with a thund'ring sound, 1015 ⎫
Iis pond'rous limbs oppress the trembling ground; ⎪
;lood, brains, and foam, gush from the gaping ⎬
[wound. ⎭

;calp, face, and shoulders, the keen steel divides;
ind the shar'd visage hangs on equal sides.
[he Trojans fly from their approaching fate: 1020
ind had the victor then secur'd the gate,
ind, to his troops without, unclos'd the bars;
)ne lucky day had ended all his wars.
]ut boiling youth, and blind desire of blood,
]ush on his fury, to pursue the crowd; 1025

Hamftring'd behind unhappy Gyges dy'd;
Then Phalaris is added to his fide:
The pointed jav'lins from the dead he drew,
And their friends arms againft their fellows threw.
Strong Halys ftands in vain; weak Phlegys flies; 1030
Saturnia, ftill at hand, new force and fire fupplies.
Then Halius, Prytanis, Alcander fall;
(Engag'd againft the foes, who fcal'd the wall:)
But whom they fear'd without, they found within:
At laft, tho' late, by Linceus he was feen.   1035
He calls new fuccours, and affaults the prince,
But weak his force, and vain is their defence.
Turn'd to the right, his fword the hero drew,
And at one blow the bold aggreffor flew.
He joints the neck: and with a ftroke fo ftrong 1040
The helm flies off; and bears the head along.
Next him, the huntfman Amycus he kill'd,
In darts, invenom'd, and in poifon fkill'd.
Then Clytius fell beneath his fatal fpear,
And Cretus, whom the mufes held fo dear: 1045
He fought with courage, and he fung the fight:
Arms were his bus'nefs, verfes his delight.
    The Trojan chiefs behold, with rage and grief,
Their flaughter'd friends, and haften their relief.

ɔld Mneſtheus rallies firſt the broken train,   1050
Ⴕhom brave Sereſthus and his troop ſuſtain.
ɔ ſave the living, and revenge the dead:
gainſt one warrior's arms all Troy they led.
, void of ſenſe and courage, Mneſtheus cry'd,
Ⴕhere can you hope your coward heads to hide? 1055
h, where beyond theſe rampires can you run!
'ne man, and in your camp incloſ'd, you ſhun!
hall then a ſingle ſword ſuch ſlaughter boaſt,
nd paſs unpuniſh'd from a num'rous hoſt?
orſaking honour, and renouncing fame,   1060
'our gods, your country, and your king you ſhame.
  This juſt reproach their virtue does excite,
hey ſtand, they join, they thicken to the fight.
  Now Turnus doubts, and yet diſdains to yield:
ut with ſlow paces meaſure back the field;   1065
nd inches to the walls, where Tiber's tide,
Vaſhing the camp, defends the weaker ſide.
he more he loſes, they advance the more;
nd tread in ev'ry ſtep he trod before.   1069
hey ſhout, they bear him back, and whom by might
hey cannot conquer, they oppreſs with weight.
  As compaſs'd with a wood of ſpears around,
he lordly lion ſtill maintains his ground;

Grins horrible, retires, and turns again ;
Threats his diftended paws, and fhakes his mane;
He lofes while in vain he preffes on,   1076
Nor will his courage let him dare to run :
So Turnus fares, and unrefolv'd of flight,
Moves tardy back, and juft recedes from fight.
Yet twice, enrag'd, the combat he renews,   1080
Twice breaks, and twice his broken foes purfues :
But now they fwarm ; and with frefh troops fupply'd,
Come rolling on, and rufh from ev'ry fide.
Nor Juno, who fuftain'd his arms before,
Dares with new ftrength fuffice, th' exhaufted ftore.
For Jove, with four commands, fent Iris down,1086
To force th' invader from the frighted town.

  With labour fpent, no longer can he wield
The heavy fauchion, or fuftain the fhield :
O'erwhelm'd with darts, which from afar they fling,
The weapons round his hollow temples ring : 1091
His golden helm gives way : with ftony blows
Batter'd, and flat, and beaten to his brows,
His creft is rafh'd away, his ample fhield
Is falfify'd, and round with jav'lins fill'd.   1095

  The foe now faint ; the Trojans overwhelm :
And Mneftheus lays hard load upon his helm.

Sick fweat fucceeds, he drops at ev'ry pore,
With driving duft his cheeks are pafted o'er.
Shorter and fhorter ev'ry gafp he takes,   1100
And vain efforts, and hurtlefs blows he makes.
Arm'd as he was, at length, he leap'd from high;
Plung'd in the flood, and made the waters fly.
The yellow god, the welcome burden bore,
And wip'd the fweat, and wafh'd away the gore:
Then gently wafts him to the farther coaft;   1105
And fends him fafe to chear his anxious hoft.

THE

TENTH BOOK

OF THE

Æ N E I S.

THE

ARGUMENT.

JUPITER calling a council of the gods, forbids them to engage in either party. At Æneas's return there is a bloody battle: Turnus killing Pallas; Æneas, Lausus and Mezentius. Mezentius is describ'd as an atheist; Lausus as a pious and virtuous youth: The different actions and death of these two, are the subject of a noble episode.

The Tenth Book of the

Æ   N   E   I   S.

THE gates of heav'n unfold; Jove summons all
    The gods to council in the common hall.
Sublimely seated he surveys from far
The fields, the camp, the fortune of the war;
And all th' inferior world: from first to last   5
The sov'reign senate in degrees are plac'd.
Then thus th' almighty sire began.   Ye gods,
Natives, or denizons, of blest abodes;
From whence these murmurs, and this change of
                       {mind,
This backward fate from what was first design'd? 10
Why this protracted war? When my commands·
Pronounc'd a peace, and gave the Latian lands.

What fear or hope on either part divides
Our heav'ns, and arms our pow'rs on diff'rent sides?
A lawful time of war at length will come,   15
(Nor need your haste anticipate the doom,)
When Carthage shall contend the world with Rome:
Shall force the rigid rocks, and Alpine chains;
And like a flood come pouring on the plains.
Then is your time for faction and debate,   20
For partial favour, and permitted hate.
Let now your immature dissension cease:
Sit quiet, and compose your souls to peace.

   Thus Jupiter in few unfolds the charge:
But lovely Venus thus replies at large.   25
O pow'r immense, eternal energy!
(For to what else protection can we fly,)
Seest thou the proud Rutulians, how they dare
In fields, unpunish'd, and insult my care?
How lofty Turnus vaunts amidst his train,   30
In shining arms triumphant on the plain?
Ev'n in their lines and trenches they contend;
And scarce their walls the Trojan troops defend:
The town is fill'd with slaughter, and o'erfloats,
With a red deluge, their increasing moats.   35
Æneas ignorant, and far from thence,
Has left a camp expos'd, without defence.

J. Collyer sculp.

This endlefs outrage fhall they ftill fuftain ?
Shall Troy renew'd be forc'd, and fir'd again ?
A fecond fiege my banifh'd iffue fears,   40
And a new Diomede in arms appears.
One more audacious mortal will be found ;
And I thy daughter wait another wound.
Yet, if with fates averfe, without thy leave,
The Latian lands my progeny receive ;   45
Bear they the pains of violated law,
And thy protection from their aid withdraw.
But if the gods their fure fuccefs foretel,
If thofe of heav'n confent with thofe of hell,
To promife Italy ; who dare debate   50
The pow'r of Jove, or fix another fate ?
What fhould I tell of tempefts on the main,
Of Eolus ufurping Neptune's reign ?
Of Iris fent ; with Bacchanalian heat,
T' infpire the matrons, and deftroy the fleet.   55
Now Juno to the Stygian fky defcends,
Solicits hell for aid, and arms the fiends.
That new example wanted yet above :
An act that well became the wife of Jove.
Alecto, rais'd by her, with rage inflames   60
The peaceful bofoms of the Latian dames.

Imperial fway no more exalts my mind :
(Such hopes I had indeed, while heav'n was kind)
Now let my happier foes poffefs my place,
Whom Jove prefers before the Trojan race;   65
And conquer they, whom you with conqueft grace.
Since you can fpare, from all your wide command,
No fpot of earth, no hofpitable land,
Which may my wand'ring fugitives receive;
(Since haughty Juno will not give you leave)   70
Then, father, (if I ftill may ufe that name)
By ruin'd Troy, yet fmoking from the flame,
I beg you let Afcanius, by my care,
Be freed from danger, and difmifs'd the war :
Inglorious let him live, without a crown;   75
The father may be caft on coafts unknown,
Struggling with fate; but let me fave the fon.
Mine is Cythera, mine the Cyprian tow'rs;
In thofe receffes, and thofe facred bow'rs
Obfcurely let him reft; his right refign   80
To promis'd empire, and his Julian line.
Then Carthage may th' Aufonian towns deftroy,
Nor fear the race of a rejected boy.
What profits it my fon, to 'fcape the fire,
Arm'd with his gods, and loaded with his fire: 85

To pass the perils of the seas and wind;
Evade the Greeks, and leave the war behind;
To reach th' Italian shores: if after all,
Our second Pergamus is doom'd to fall?
Much better had he curb'd his high desires,   90
And hover'd o'er his ill-extinguish'd fires.
To Simois' banks the fugitives restore,
And give them back to war, and all the woes before.

　　Deep indignation swell'd Saturnia's heart:
And must I own, she said, my secret smart?   95
What with more decence were in silence kept,
And but for this unjust reproach had slept.
Did god, or man, your fav'rite son advise,
With war unhop'd the Latians to surprise?
By fate you boast, and by the gods decree,   100
He left his native land for Italy:
Confess the truth; by mad Cassandra, more
Than heav'n inspir'd, he sought a foreign shore!
Did I persuade to trust his second Troy,
To the raw conduct of a beardless boy?   105
With walls unfinish'd, which himself forsakes,
And thro' the waves a wand'ring voyage takes?
When have I urg'd him meanly to demand
The Tuscan aid, and arm a quiet land?

Did I or Iris give this mad advice,　　　110
Or made the fool himſelf the fatal choice?
You think it hard, the Latians ſhould deſtroy
With ſwords your Trojans, and with fires your Troy:
Hard and unjuſt indeed, for men to draw
Their native air, nor take a foreign law:　　115
That Turnus is permitted ſtill to live,
To whom his birth a god and goddeſs give:
But yet 'tis juſt and lawful for your line,
To drive their fields, and force with fraud to join.
Realms not your own, among your clans divide, 120
And from the bridegroom tear the promis'd bride:
Petition, while you publick arms prepare;
Pretend a peace, and yet provoke a war.
'Twas giv'n to you, your darling ſon to ſhroud,
To draw the daſtard from the fighting crowd;　125
And for a man obtend an empty cloud.
From flaming fleets you turn'd the fire away,
And chang'd the ſhips to daughters of the ſea.
But 'tis my crime, the queen of heav'n offends,
If ſhe preſume to ſave her ſuff'ring friends.　130
Your ſon, not knowing what his foes decree,
You ſay is abſent: abſent let him be.
Yours is Cythera, yours the Cyprian tow'rs,
The ſoft receſſes, and the ſacred bow'rs.

Why do you then thefe needlefs arms prepare,   135
And thus provoke a people prone to war?
Did I with fire the Trojan town deface,
Or hinder from return your exil'd race?
Was I the caufe of mifchief, or the man,
Whofe lawlefs luft the fatal war began?   140
Think on whofe faith th' adult'rous youth rely'd:
Who promis'd, who procur'd the Spartan bride?
When all th' united ftates of Greece combin'd,
To purge the world of the perfidious kind;
Then was your time to fear the Trojan fate: 145
Your quarrels and complaints are now too late.

  Thus Juno. Murmurs rife, with mix'd applaufe;
Juft as they favour, or diflike the caufe:
So winds, when yet unfledg'd in woods they lie,
In whifpers firft their tender voices try: 150
Then iffue on the main with bellowing rage,
And ftorms to trembling mariners prefage.

  Then thus to both reply'd th' imperial god,
Who fhakes heav'n's axles with his awful nod.
(When he begins, the filent fenate ftand   155
With rev'rence, lift'ning to the dread command:
The clouds difpel; the winds their breath reftrain,
And the hufh'd waves lie flatted on the main.)

D 6

Cœleftials ! your attentive ears incline ;
Since, faid the god, the Trojans muft not join   160
In wifh'd alliance with the Latian line,

Since endlefs jarrings, and immortal hate,
Tend but to difcompofe our happy ftate ;
The war henceforward be refign'd to Fate,
Each to his proper fortune ftand or fall,   165
Equal and unconcern'd I look on all.

Rutulians, Trojans, are the fame to me ;
And both fhall draw the lots their fates decree.
Let thefe affault ; if fortune be their friend ;
And if fhe favours thofe, let thofe defend :   170
The Fates will find their way. The thund'rer faid ;
And fhook the facred honours of his head ;
Attefting Styx, th' inviolable flood,
And the black regions of his brother god :
Trembled the poles of heav'n ; and earth confefs'd
                                    [the nod :
This end the feffions had : the fenate rife,   176
And to his palace wait their fov'reign thro' the fkies.

    Mean time, intent upon their fiege, the foes
Within their walls the Trojan hoft inclofe :
They wound, they kill, they watch at ev'ry gate : 180
Renew the fires, and urge their happy fate.

Th' Æneans wifh in vain their wanted chief,
Hopelefs of flight, more hopelefs of relief;
Thin on the tow'rs they ftand; and'ev'n thofe few,
A feeble, fainting, and dejected crew :   185
Yet in the face of danger fome there ftood :
The two bold brothers of Sarpedon's blood,
Afius and Acmon : both th' Affaraci ;
Young Hæmon, and tho' young, refolv'd to die.
With thefe were Clarus and Thymetes join'd; 190
Tibris and Caftor, both of Lycian kind.
From Acmon's hands a rolling ftone there came,
So large, it half deferv'd a mountain's name !
Strong-finew'd was the youth, and big of bone, ⎫
His brother Mneftheus cou'd not more have done: ⎬
Or the great father of th' intrepid fon.   196 ⎭
Some firebrands throw, fome flights of arrows fend ;
And fome with darts, and fome with ftones defend.
Amid the prefs appears the beauteous boy,
The care of Venus, and the hope of Troy.   200
His lovely face unarm'd, his head was bare,
In ringlets o'er his fhoulders hung his hair.
His forehead circled with a diadem ;
Diftinguifh'd from the crowd he fhines a gem,
Enchas'd in gold, or polifh'd iv'ry fet,   205
Amidft the meaner foil of fable jet.

Nor Ismarus was wanting to the war,
Directing pointed arrows from afar,
And death with poison arm'd: in Lydia born,
Where plenteous harvests the fat fields adorn :   210
Where proud Pactolus floats the fruitful lands,
And leaves a rich manure of golden sands.
There Capys, author of the Capuan name:
And there was Mnestheus too increas'd in fame : 214
Since Turnus from the camp he cast with shame.
    Thus mortal war was wag'd on either side.
Mean time the hero cuts the nightly tide :
For, anxious, from Evander when he went,
He sought the Tyrrhene camp, and Tarchon's tent;
Expos'd the cause of coming to the chief;   220
His name and country told, and ask'd relief :
Propos'd the terms; his own small strength declar'd,
What vengeance proud Mezentius had prepar'd :
What Turnus, bold and violent design'd ;
Then shew'd the slipp'ry state of human kind,   225
And fickle fortune; warn'd him to beware:
And to his wholsom counsel added pray'r.
Tarchon, without delay, the treaty signs ;
And to the Trojan troops the Tuscan joins.   229
    They soon set fail; nor now the fates withstand ;
Their forces trusted with a foreign hand.

Æneas leads; upon his ſtern appear
Two lions carv'd, which riſing Ida bear;
Ida, to wand'ring Trojans ever dear.
Under their grateful ſhade Æneas ſate,   235.
Revolving wars events, and various fate.
His left young Pallas kept, fix'd to his ſide,
And oft of winds enquir'd, and of the tide:
Oft of the ſtars, and of their wat'ry way;
And what he ſuffer'd both by land and ſea.   240

Now ſacred ſiſters open all your ſpring,
The Tuſcan leaders, and their army ſing;
Which follow'd great Æneas to the war:
Their arms, their numbers, and their names declare.

A thouſand youths brave Maſſicus obey,   245.
Born in the Tiger, thro' the foaming ſea;
From Aſium brought, and Coſa, by his care;
For arms, light quivers, bows and ſhafts they bear.
Fierce Abas next, his men bright armour wore;
His ſtern, Apollo's golden ſtatue bore.   250
Six hundred Populonea ſent along,
All ſkill'd in martial exerciſe, and ſtrong.
Three hundred more for battle Ilva joins,
An iſle renown'd for ſteel, and unexhauſted mines.
Aſylas on his prow the third appears,   255
Who heav'n interprets, and the wand'ring ſtars:

From offer'd entrails prodigies expounds,
And peals of thunder, with prefaging founds.
A thoufand fpears in warlike order ftand,
Sent by the Pifans under his command.   260
 Fair Aftur follows in the wat'ry field,
Proud of his manag'd horfe, and painted fhield..
Gravifca noifom from the neighb'ring fen,
And his own Cœre fent three hundred men :
With thofe which Minio's fields, and Pyrgi gave.;.
All bred in arms, unanimous and brave.   266
 Thou mufe the name of Cinyras renew ;
And brave Cupavo follow'd but by few :
Whofe helm confefs'd the lineage of the man,
And bore, with wings difplay'd, a filver fwan. 270
Love was the fault of his fam'd anceftry,
Whofe forms, and fortunes in his enfigns fly.
For Cycnus lov'd unhappy Phaeton,
And fung his lofs in poplar groves, alone ;.
Beneath the fifter fhades to footh his grief :   275.
Heav'n heard his fong, and haften'd his relief :
And chang'd to fnowy plumes his hoary hair,.
And wing'd his flight, to chant aloft in air.
His fon Cupavo brufh'd the briny flood :
Upon his ftern a brawny centaur ftood,   280

Who heav'd a rock, and threat'ning ftill to throw,
With lifted hands, alarm'd the feas below:
They feem to fear the formidable fight,
And roll'd their billows on, to fpeed his flight.

Ocnus was next, who led his native train,   285
Of hardy warriors thro' the wat'ry plain,
The fon of Manto, by the Tufcan ftream,
From whence the Mantuan town derives the name,
An ancient city, but of mix'd defcent,
Three feveral tribes compofe the government;   290
Four towns are under each; but all obey
The Mantuan laws, and own the Tufcan fway.

Hate to Mezentius, arm'd five hundred more,
Whom Mincius from his fire Benacus bore;   294
(Mincius with wreaths of reeds his forehead co-
                              [ver'd o'er.)

Thefe grave Auletes leads. A hundred fweep,
With ftretching oars at once the glafly deep:
Him, and his martial train, the Triton bears,
High on his poop the fea-green god appears:
Frowning he feems his crooked fhell to found,   300
And at the blaft the billows dance around.
A hairy man above the waift he fhows,
A porpoife tail beneath his belly grows;

And ends a fish : his breast the waves divides,
And froth and foam augment the murm'ring tides.

    Full thirty ships transport the chosen train, 306
For Troy's relief, and scour the briny main.

    Now was the world forsaken by the sun,
And Phœbe half her nightly race had run.
The careful chief, who never clos'd his eyes, 310
Himself the rudder holds, the sails supplies.
A choir of Nereids meet him on the flood,
Once his own gallies, hewn from Ida's wood :
But now as many nymphs the sea they sweep,
As rode before tall vessels on the deep.   315
They know him from afar ; and in a ring
Inclose the ship that bore the Trojan king.
Cymodoce, whose voice excell'd the rest,
Above the waves advanc'd her snowy breast.
Her right hand stops the stern, her left divides 320
The curling ocean, and corrects the tides :
She spoke for all the choir ; and thus began
With pleasing words to warn th' unknowing man.
Sleeps our lov'd lord ? O goddess-born ! awake,
Spread ev'ry sail, pursue your wat'ry track ; 325
And haste your course.   Your navy once were we,
From Ida's height descending to the sea :

Till Turnus, as at anchor fix'd we ftood,
Prefum'd to violate our holy wood.
Then loos'd from fhore we fled his fires profane;
(Unwillingly we broke our mafter's chain)   331 }
And fince have fought you thro' the Tufcan main.
The mighty mother chang'd our forms to thefe,
And gave us life immortal in the feas.
But young Afcanius, in his camp diftrefs'd,   335
By your infulting foes is hardly prefs'd,
Th' Areadian horfemen, and Etrurian hoft
Advance in order on the Latian coaft:
To cut their way the Daunian chief defigns,
Before their troops can reach the Trojan lines.   340
Thou, whom the rofy morn reftores the light,
Firft arm thy foldiers for th' enfuing fight;
Thyfelf the fated fword of Vulcan wield,
And bear aloft th' impenetrable fhield.
To-morrow's fun, unlefs my fkill be vain,   345
Shall fee huge heaps of foes in battle flain.
Parting, fhe fpoke; and with immortal force,
Pufh'd on the veffel in her wat'ry courfe:
(For well fhe knew the way) impell'd behind,
The fhip flew forward, and outftript the wind.   350
The reft make up: unknowing of the caufe;
The chief admires their fpeed, and happy omens draws.

Then thus he pray'd, and fix'd on heaven his eyes;
Hear thou, great mother of the deities,
With turrets crown'd, (on Ida's holy hill,   355
Fierce tygers, rein'd and curb'd, obey thy will.)
Firm thy own omens, lead us on to fight,
And let thy Phrygians conquer in thy right.

He said no more.   And now renewing day
Had chas'd the shadows of the night away.   360
He charg'd the soldiers with preventing care,
Their flags to follow, and their arms prepare;
Warn'd of th' ensuing fight, and bad 'em hope the
                              [war.

Now from his lofty poop, he view'd below,
His camp encompass'd, and th' inclosing foe.   365
His blazing shield embrac'd, he held on high;
The camp receive the sign, and with loud shouts reply.
Hope arms their courage: from their tow'rs they throw
Their darts with double force, and drive the foe.
Thus, at the signal giv'n, the cranes arise   370
Before the stormy south, and blacken all the skies.

King Turnus wonder'd at the fight renew'd;
Till, looking back, the Trojan fleet he view'd;
The seas with swelling canvass cover'd o'er;
And the swift ships descending on the shore.   375

The Latians faw from far, with dazled eyes,
The radiant creft that feem'd in flames to rife,
And dart diffufive fires around the field;
And the keen glitt'ring of the golden fhield.   379

   Thus threat'ning comets, when by night they rife,
Shoot fanguine ftreams, and fadden all the fkies:
So Sirius, flafhing forth finifter lights,
Pale human kind with plagues, and with dry famine
                                                   [frights.

Yet Turnus, with undaunted mind is bent
To man the fhores, and hinder their defcent: 385
And thus awakes the courage of his friends.
What you fo long have wifh'd, kind fortune fends:
In ardent arms to meet th' invading foe:
You find, and find him at advantage now.

Yours is the day, you need but only dare: 390
Your fwords will make you mafters of the war.
Your fires, your fons, your houfes, and your lands,
And deareft wives, are all within your hands.
Be mindful of the race from whence you came;
And emulate in arms your father's fame.   395
Now take the time, while ftagg'ring yet they ftand
With feet unfirm; and prepoffefs the ftrand:
Fortune befriends the bold.   No more he faid,
But balanc'd whom to leave, and whom to lead:

Then thefe elects, the landing to prevent;   400
And thofe he leaves to keep the city pent.

    Mean time the Trojan fends his troops afhore:
Some are by boats expos'd, by bridges more.
With lab'ring oars they bear along the ftrand,
Where the tide languifhes, and leap a-land.   405
Tarchon obferves the coaft with careful eyes,
And where no ford he finds, no water fries,
Nor billows with unequal murmur roar,
But fmoothly flide along, and fwell the fhore;
That courfe he fteer'd, and thus he gave command,
Here ply your oars, and at all hazard land: 411
Force on the veffel, that her keel may wound
This hated foil, and furrow hoftile ground;
Let me fecurely land, I afk no more,
Then fink my fhips, or fhatter on the fhore;   415
This fiery fpeech inflames his fearful friends,
They tug at ev'ry oar; and ev'ry ftretcher bends:
They run their fhips aground, the veffels knock,
(Thus forc'd afhore) and tremble with the fhock.
Tarchon's alone was loft, and ftranded ftood,   420
Stuck on a bank, and beaten by the flood.
She breaks her back, the loofen'd fides give way,
And plunge the Tufcan foldiers in the fea.

Their broken oars, and floating planks withstand
Their passage, while they labour to the land;   425
And ebbing tides bear back upon th' uncertain sand.

Now Turnus leads his troops, without delay,
Advancing tow'rds the margin of the sea.
The trumpets sound: Æneas first assail'd   429
The clowns new rais'd and raw; and soon prevail'd.
Great Theron fell, an omen of the fight:
Great Theron large of limbs, of giant height.
He first in open fields defy'd the prince,
But armour scal'd with gold was no defence
Against the fated sword, which open'd wide   435
His plated shield, and pierc'd his naked side.

Next, Lycas fell; who, not like others born,
Was from his wretched mother rip'd and torn:
Sacred, O Phœbus! from his birth to thee,
For his beginning life from biting steel was free. 440
Not far from him was Gyas laid along,
Of monst'rous bulk; with Cisseus fierce and strong;
Vain bulk and strength; for when the chief assail'd,
Nor valour, nor Herculean arms avail'd;
Nor their fam'd father, wont in war to go   445
With great Alcides, while he toil'd below.
The noisy Pharos next receiv'd his death,
Æneas writh'd his dart, and stopp'd his bawling breath.

Then wretched Cydon had receiv'd his doom,
Who courted Clytius in his beardless bloom,   450
And fought with lust obscene polluted joys:
The Trojan sword had cur'd his love of boys,
Had not his seven bold brethren stop'd the course
Of the fierce champion, with united force.
Sev'n darts are thrown at once, and some rebound 455
From his bright shield, some on his helmet found :
The rest had reach'd him, but his mother's care
Prevented those, and turn'd aside in air.

   The prince then call'd Achates to supply
The spears that knew the way to victory.   460
Those fatal weapons, which inur'd to blood,
In Grecian bodies under Ilium stood :
Not one of those my hand shall toss in vain
Against our foes, on this contended plain.
He said : then seiz'd a mighty spear, and threw ; 465
Which, wing'd with fate, thro' Mæon's buckler flew:
Pierc'd all the brazen plates, and reach'd his heart :
He stagger'd with intolerable smart.
Alcanor saw ; and reach'd, but reach'd in vain,
His helping hand, his brother to sustain.   470
A second spear, which kept the former course,
From the same hand, and sent with equal force.

His right arm pierc'd, and holding on, bereft
His use of both, and pinion'd down his left.
Then Numitor, from his dead brother drew   475
The ill-omen'd spear, and at the Trojan threw:
Preventing fate directs the lance awry,
Which glancing, only mark'd Achates' thigh.

In pride of youth the Sabine Clausus came,
And from afar, at Dryops took his aim.   480
The spear flew hissing thro' the middle space,
And pierc'd his throat, directed at his face:
It stop'd at once the passage of his wind,
And the free soul to flitting air resign'd:
His forehead was the first that struck the ground;   485
Life-blood and life rush'd mingled thro' the wound.
He slew three brothers of the Borean race,
And three, whom Ismarus, their native place,
Had sent to war, but all the sons of Thrace.
Halesus next, the bold Aurunci leads;   490
The son of Neptune to his aid succeeds,
Conspicuous on his horse: on either hand
These fight to keep, and those to win the land.
With mutual blood th' Ausonian soil is dy'd,
While on its borders each their claim decide.   495

As wintry winds contending in the ſky,
With equal force of lungs their titles try :
They rage, they roar; the doubtful rack of heav'n
Stands without motion, and the tide undriv'n :
Each bent to conquer, neither ſide to yield ;   500
They long ſuſpend the fortune of the field.
Both armies thus perform what courage can :
Foot ſet to foot, and mingled man to man.

But in another part, th' Arcadian horſe,
With ill-ſucceſs engage the Latian force.   505
For where th' impetuous torrent ruſhing down,
Huge craggy ſtones, and rooted trees had thrown :
They left their courſers, and unus'd to fight
On foot, were ſcatter'd in a ſhameful flight.
Pallas, who with diſdain and grief, had view'd   510
His foes purſuing, and his friends purſu'd ;
Us'd threatnings mix'd with pray'rs, his laſt reſource;
With theſe to move their minds, with thoſe to fire
[their force.
Which way, companions! whither wou'd you run!
By you yourſelves, and mighty battles won;   516
By my great ſire, by his eſtabliſh'd name,
And early promiſe of my future fame ;
By my youth emulous of equal right,
To ſhare his honours, ſhun ignoble flight.   520

Truft not your feet, your hands muft hew your way
Thro' yon black body,. and that thick array :
'Tis thro' that forward path that we muft come :
There lies our way, and that our paffage home.
Nor pow'rs above, nor deftinies below,   525
Opprefs our arms; with equal ftrength we go;
With mortal hands to meet a mortal foe.
See on what foot we ftand : a fcanty fhore ;
The fea behind, our enemies before :
No paffage left, unlefs we fwim the main ;
Or forcing thefe, the Trojan trenches gain.   530
This faid, he ftrode with eager hafte along,
And bore amidft the thickeft of the throng.
Lagus, the firft he met, with fate to foe,
Had heav'd a ftone of mighty weight to throw ;
Stooping, the fpear defcended on his chine,   535
Juft where the bone diftinguifh'd either loin :
It ftuck fo faft, fo deeply bury'd lay,
That fcarce the victor forc'd the fteel away.
Hifbon came on, but while he mov'd too flow
To wifh'd revenge, the prince prevents his blow; 540
For warding his at once, at once he prefs'd ;
And plung'd the fatal weapon in his breaft.

E 2

'Then leud Anchemolus he laid in duft,
Who ftain'd his ftepdam's bed with impious luft,
And after him the Daunian twins were flain,   545
Laris and Thimbrus, on the Latian plain :
So wond'rous like in feature, fhape, and fize,
As caus'd an error in their parents eyes.
Grateful miftake! but foon the fword decides
The nice diftinction, and their fate divides.   550
For Thimbrus' head was lop'd : and Laris' hand
Difmember'd, fought its owner on the ftrand :
The trembling fingers yet the fauchion ftrain,
And threaten ftill th' intended ftroke in vain.   554

    Now, to renew the charge, th' Arcadians came,
Sight of fuch acts, and fenfe of honeft fhame,
And grief, with anger mix'd, their minds inflame.
Then, with a cafual blow was Rhæteus flain,
Who chanc'd, as Pallas threw, to crofs the plain !
The flying fpear was after Ilus fent,   560
But Rhæteus happen'd on a death unmeant :
From Teuthras, and from Tyrus while he fled,
The lance, athwart his body, laid him dead.
Roll'd from his chariot with a mortal wound,
And intercepted fate, he fpurn'd the ground.   565

    As when in fummer, welcome winds arife,
The watchful fhepherd to the foreft flies,

And fires the midmoſt plants; contagion ſpreads,
And catching flames infeſt the neighb'ring heads;
Around the foreſt flies the furious blaſt,   570
And all the leafy nation ſinks at laſt;
And Vulcan rides in triumph o'er the waſte:
The paſtor pleas'd with his dire victory,
Beholds the ſatiate flames in ſheets aſcend the ſky:
So Pallas' troops their ſcatter'd ſtrength unite; 575
And pouring on their foes, their prince delight.

  Haleſus came, fierce with deſire of blood,
(But firſt collected in his arms he ſtood)
Advancing then he ply'd the ſpear ſo well,
Ladon, Demodochus, and Pheres fell: 580
Around his head he toſs'd his glitt'ring brand,
And from Strymonius hew'd his better hand,
Held up to guard his throat: then hurl'd a ſtone
At Thoas' ample front, and pierc'd the bone:
It ſtruck beneath the ſpace of either eye,   585
And blood, and mingled brains, together fly.
Deep ſkill'd in future fates, Haleſus' ſire,
Did with the youth to lonely groves retire:
But when the father's mortal race was run,
Dire Deſtiny laid hold upon the ſon,   590

                E 3

And haul'd him to the war : to find beneath
Th' Evandrian fpear, a memorable death.
Pallas th' encounter feeks, but ere he'throws,
To Tufcan Tiber thus addrefs'd his vows :
O facred ftream, direct my flying dart ;   595
And give to pafs the proud Halefus' heart :
His arms and fpoils thy holy oak fhall bear.
Pleas'd with the bribe, the god receiv'd his pray'r.
For while his fhield protects a friend diftrefs'd,
The dart came driving on, and pierc'd his breaft. 600

But Laufus, no fmall portion of the war,
Permits not panick fear to reign too far,
Caus'd by the death of fo renown'd a knight :
But by his own example chears the fight.
Fierce Abas firft he flew, Abas, the ftay   605
Of Trojan hopes, and hind'rance of the day.
The Phrygian troops efcap'd the Greeks in vain,
They, and their mix'd allies, now lead the plain.
To the rude fhock of war both armies came,
The leaders equal, and their ftrength the fame. 610
The rear fo prefs'd the front, they could not wield
Their angry weapons, to difpute the field.
Here Pallas urges on, and Laufus there,
Of equal youth and beauty both appear,   615
But both by fate forbid to breathe their native air.

Their congrefs in the field great Jove withftands,
Both doom'd to fall, but fall by greater hands.

Mean time Juturna warns the Daunian chief
Of Laufus' danger, urging fwift relief.
With his driv'n chariot he divides the crowd,   620
And making to his friends, thus calls aloud ;
Let none prefume his needlefs aid to join ;
Retire, and clear the field, the fight is mine :
To this right hand is Pallas only due :
Oh were his father here my juft revenge to view !
From the forbidden fpace his men retir'd ;   626
Pallas, their awe, and his ftern words admir'd :
Survey'd him o'er and o'er with wond'ring fight,
Struck with his haughty mien, and tow'ring height-
Then to the king; your empty vaunts forbear;   630
Succefs I hope, and Fate I cannot fear.
Alive or dead, I fhall deferve a name :
Jove is impartial, and to both the fame.
He faid, and to the void advanc'd his pace ;
Pale horror fat on each Arcadian face.   635
Then Turnus, from his chariot leaping light,
Addrefs'd himfelf on foot to fingle fight.
And, as a lion, when he fpies from far
A bull that feems to meditate the war ;

Bending his neck, and spurning back the sand, 640
Runs roaring downward from his hilly stand :
Imagine eager Turnus not more slow,
To rush from high on his unequal foe.

    Young Pallas, when he saw the chief advance
Within due distance of his flying lance;   645
Prepares to charge him first : resolv'd to try
If Fortune wou'd his want of force supply.
And thus to heav'n and Hercules addrefs'd.
Alcides, once on earth Evander's guest,
His son adjures you by those holy rites,   650
That hospitable board, those genial nights;
Affist my great attempt to gain this prize,
And let proud Turnus view, with dying eyes,
His ravish'd spoils. 'Twas heard, the vain requeft;
Alcides mourn'd; and ftifled fighs within his breaft;
Then Jove, to footh his forrow, thus began, 656 ⎫
Short bounds of life are fet to mortal man.   ⎬
'Tis virtue's work alone to ftretch the narrow fpan. ⎭
So many fons of gods in bloody fight,
Around the walls of Troy, have loft the light: 660
My own Sarpedon fell beneath his foe,
Nor I, his mighty fire, cou'd ward the blow.
Ev'n Turnus fhortly fhall refign his breath;
And ftands already on the verge of death.

This faid, the god permits the fatal fight,   665
But from the Latian fields averts his fight.

Now with full force his fpear young Pallas threw;
And having thrown, his fhining fauchion drew:
The fteel juft graz'd along the fhoulder joint,
And mark'd it flightly with the glancing point. 670
Fierce Turnus firft to nearer diftance drew,
And pois'd his pointed fpear before he threw:
Then, as the winged weapon whiz'd along;
See now, faid he, whofe arm is better ftrung.
The fpear kept on the fatal courfe, unftay'd   675
By plates of iron, which o'er the fhield were laid:
Thro' folded brafs, and tough bull-hides it pafs'd,
His croflet pierc'd, and reach'd his heart at laft.
In vain the youth tugs at the broken wood,
The foul comes iffuing with the vital blood: 680
He falls; his arms upon his body found;
And with his bloody teeth he bites the ground.

Turnus beftrode the corps: Arcadians hear,
Said he; my meffage to your mafter bear:
Such as the fire deferv'd, the fon I fe d: 685
It cofts him dear to be the Phrygians' friend.
The lifelefs body, tell him, I beftow
Unafk'd, to reft his wand'ring ghoft below.

E. 5

He ſaid, and trampled down with all the force
Of his left foot, and ſpurn'd the wretched corſe : 690
Then ſnatch'd the ſhining belt, with gold inlaid;
The belt Eurytion's artful hands had made :
Where fifty fatal brides, expreſs'd to ſight,
All, in the compaſs of one mournful night,
Depriv'd their bridegrooms of returning light. 695

　In an ill hour inſulting Turnus tore
Thoſe golden ſpoils, and in a worſe he wore.
O mortals ! blind in fate, who never know
To bear high fortune, or endure the low !
The time ſhall come, when Turnus, but in vain, 700
Shall wiſh untouch'd the trophies of the ſlain :
Shall wiſh the fatal belt were far away ;
And curſe the dire remembrance of the day.

　The ſad Arcadians from th' unhappy field,
Bear back the breathleſs body on a ſhield. 705
O grace and grief of war ! at once reſtor'd
With praiſes to thy ſire, at once deplor'd.
One day firſt ſent thee to the fighting field,
Beheld whole heaps of foes in battle kill'd ; 710
One day beheld thee dead, and born upon thy ſhield.
This diſmal news, not from uncertain fame,
But ſad ſpectators, to the hero came :

His friends upon the brink of ruin ftand,
Unlefs reliev'd by his victorious hand.
He whirls his fword around, without delay,   715
And hews through adverfe foes an ample way;
To find fierce Turnus, of his conqueft proud :
Evander, Pallas, all that friendfhip ow'd
To large deferts, are prefent to his eyes;
His plighted hand, and hofpitable ties.   720

   Four fons of Sulmo, four whom Ufens bred,
He took in fight, and living victims led,
To pleafe the ghoft of Pallas; and expire
In facrifice, before his fun'ral fire.
At Magus next he threw : he ftoop'd below   725
The flying fpear, and fhun'd the promis'd blow.
Then creeping, clafp'd the hero's knees, and pray'd :
By young Iulus, by thy father's fhade,
O fpare my life, and fend me back to fee
My longing fire, and tender progeny.   730
A lofty houfe I have, and wealth untold,
In filver ingots, and in bars of gold :
All thefe, and fums befides, which fee no day,
The ranfom of this one poor life fhall pay.
If I furvive, fhall Troy the lefs prevail ?   735
A fingle foul's too light to turn the fcale.

E 6.

He faid.   The hero fternly thus reply'd :
Thy bars, and ingots, and the fums befide,
Leave for thy childrens lot.   Thy Turnus broke
All rules of war, by one relentlefs ftroke,   740
When Pallas fell : fo deems, nor deems alone,
My father's fhadow, but my living fon.
Thus having faid, of kind remorfe bereft,
He feiz'd his helm, and dragg'd him with his left:
Then with his right hand, while his neck he wreath'd,
Up to the hilts his fhining fauchion fheath'd.   746

 Apollo's prieft, Hæmonides was near,
His holy fillets on his front appear ;
Glitt'ring in arms he fhone amidft the crow'd ;
Much of his god, more of his purple proud :   750
Him the fierce Trojan follow'd thro' the field,
The holy coward fell : and forc'd to yield,
The prince ftood o'er the prieft ; and at one blow,
Sent him an off'ring to the fhades below.
His arms Serefthus on his fhoulders bears,   755
Defign'd a trophee to the god of wars.

 Vulcanian Cæculus renews the fight ;
And Umbro born upon the mountain's height.
The champion chears his troops t'encounter thofe ;
And feeks revenge himfelf on other foes.   760

At Anxur's fhield he drove, and at the blow,
Both fhield and arm to ground together go.
Anxur had boafted much of magic charms,
And thought he wore impénetrable arms;
So made by mutter'd fpells: and from the fpheres, 765
Had life fecur'd in vain, for length of years.
Then Tarquitus the field in triumph trod;
A nymph his mother, and his fire a god.
Exulting in bright arms he braves the prince;
With his protended lance he makes defence: 770
Bears back his feeble foe; then preffing on,
Arrefts his better hand, and drags him down.
Stands o'er the proftrate wretch, and as he lay,
Vain tales inventing, and prepar'd to pray,
Mows off his head; the trunk a moment ftood, 775
Then funk, and roll'd along the fand in blood.
   The vengeful victor thus upbraids the flain;
Lie there, proud man, unpity'd on the plain:
Lie there, inglorious, and without a tomb,
Far from thy mother, and thy native home: 780
Expos'd to favage beafts, and birds of prey;
Or thrown for food to monfters of the fea.
   On Lycas and Antæus next he ran,
Two chiefs of Turnus, and who led his van.

They fled for fear; with thefe he chas'd along, 785
Camers the yellow-look'd, and Numa ftrong,
Both great in arms, and both were fair and young:
Camers was fon to Volfcens lately flain;
In wealth furpaffing all the Latian train,
And in Amycla fix'd his filent eafy reign.   790

     And as Ægean, when with heaven he ftrove,
Stood oppofite in arms to mighty Jove;
Mov'd all his hundred hands, provok'd the war,
Defy'd the forky lightning from afar:
At fifty mouths his flaming breath expires,   795
And flafh for flafh returns, and fires for fires:
In his right hand as many fwords he wields,
And takes the thunder on as many fhields:
With ftrength like his the Trojan hero ftood,   799
And foon the fields with falling crops were ftrow'd,
When once his fauchion found the tafte of blood.
With fury fcarce to be conceiv'd, he flew
Againft Niphæus, whom four courfers drew.
They when they fee the fiery chief advance,
And pufhing at their chefts his pointed lance;   805
Wheel'd with fo fwift a motion, mad with fear,
They drew their mafter headlong from the chair:
They ftare, they ftart, nor ftop their courfe, before
They bear the bounding chariot to the fhore.

Now Lucagus, and Liger scour the plains, 810
With two white steeds, but Liger holds the reins,
And Lucagus the lofty seat maintains.
Bold brethren both, the former wav'd in air
His flaming sword ; Æneas couch'd his spear,
Unus'd to threats, and more unus'd to fear.　815
Then Liger thus.　Thy confidence is vain
To scape from hence, as from the Trojan plain :
Nor these the steeds which Diomede bestrode,
Nor this the chariot where Achilles rode :
Nor Venus' veil is here, nor Neptune's shield : 820
Thy fatal hour is come ; and this the field.
Thus Liger vainly vaunts : the Trojan peer
Return'd his answer with his flying spear.
As Lucagus to lash his horses bends,
Prone to the wheels, and his left foot protends, 825
Prepar'd for fight, the fatal dart arrives,
And thro' the border of his buckler drives ;
Pass'd thro' and pierc'd his groin ; the deadly wound,
Cast from his chariot, roll'd him on the ground,
Whom thus the chief upbraids with scornful spight :
Blame not the slowness of your steeds in flight ; 831
Vain shadows did not force their swift retreat :
But you yourself forsake your empty seat.

He faid, and feiz'd at once the loofen'd rein,.

(For Liger lay already on the plain   835

By the fame fhock) then ftretching out his hands,

The recreant thus his wretched life demands.

Now by thyfelf, O more than mortal man !

By her and him from whom thy breath began,.

Who form'd thee thus divine, I beg thee fpare   840

This forfeit life, and hear thy fuppliant's pray'r.

Thus much he fpoke, and more he wou'd have faid,.

But the ftern hero turn'd afide his head,

And cut him fhort. . I.hear another man,.

You talk'd not thus before the fight began ;   845

Now take your turn : and, as a brother fhou'd,

Attend your brother to the Stygian flood :

Then thro' his breaft his fatal fword he fent,.

And the foul iffu'd at the gaping vent. .

As ftorms the fkies, and torrents tear the ground, 850

Thus rag'd the prince, and fcatter'd deaths around:.

At length Afcanius, and the Trojan train,

Broke from the camp, fo long befieg'd in vain.

Mean time the king of gods and mortal man,

Held conf'rence with his queen, and thus began : 855

My fifter-goddefs, and well-pleafing wife,

Still think you Venus' aid fupports the ftrife ;.

Suftains her Trojans, or themfelves alone,
With inborn valour force their fortune on?
How fierce in fight, with courage undecay'd! 860
Judge if fuch warriors want immortal aid.
To whom the goddefs with the charming eyes,
Soft in her tone fubmiffively replies.
Why, O my fov'reign lord, whofe frown I fear,
And cannot, unconcern'd, your anger bear;   865
Why urge you thus my grief? when if I ftill
(As once I was) were miftrefs of your will:
From your almighty pow'r, your pleafing wife
Might gain the grace of length'ning Turnus' life:
Securely fnatch him from the fatal fight,   870
And give him to his aged father's fight.
Now let him perifh, fince you hold it good,
And glut the Trojans with his pious blood.
Yet from our lineage he derives his name,   874
And in the fourth degree, from god Pilumnus came!
Yet he devoutly pays you rites divine,
And offers daily incenfe at your fhrine.
    Then fhortly thus the fov'reign god reply'd;
Since in my power and goodnefs you confide;
If for a little fpace, a lengthen'd fpan,   880
You beg reprieve for this expiring man:

I grant you leave to take your Turnus hence,
From inftant fate, and can fo far difpenfe.
But if fome fecret meaning lies beneath,
To fave the fhort-liv'd youth from deftin'd death : 885
Or if a farther thought you entertain,
To change the fates; you feed your hopes in vain.

To whom the goddefs thus, with weeping eyes.
And what if that requeft your tongue denies,
Your heart fhou'd grant? and not a fhort reprieve, 890
But length of certain life to Turnus give.
Now fpeedy death attends the guiltlefs youth,
If my prefaging foul divines with truth.
Which, O! I wifh might err thro' caufelefs fears,
And you, (for you have pow'r) prolong his years. 895

Thus having faid, involv'd in clouds, fhe flies,
And drives a ftorm before her thro' the fkies.
Swift fhe defcends, alighting on the plain,
Where the fierce foes a dubious fight maintain.
Of air condens'd, a fpectre foon fhe made, 900
And what Æneas was, fuch feem'd the fhade.
Adorn'd with Dardan arms, the phantom bore
His head aloft, a plumy creft he wore :
This hand appear'd a fhining fword to wield,
And that fuftain'd an imitated fhield : 905

With manly mien he ftalk'd along the ground;
Nor wanted voice bely'd, nor vaunting found.
(Thus haunting ghofts appear to waking fight,
Or dreadful vifions in our dreams by night.)
The fpectre feems the Daunian chief to dare,   910
And flourifhes his empty fword in air:
At this advancing Turnus hurl'd his fpear;
The phantom wheel'd, and feem'd to fly for fear.
Deluded Turnus thought the Trojan fled,
And with vain hopes his haughty fancy fed.   915
Whither, O coward, (thus he calls aloud,
Nor found he fpoke to wind, and chas'd a cloud;)
Why thus forfake your bride! Receive from me
The fated land you fought fo long by fea.
He faid, and brandifhing at once his blade,   920
With eager pace purfu'd the flying fhade.
By chance a fhip was faften'd to the fhore,
Which from old Clufium king Ofinius bore:
The plank was ready laid for fafe afcent;
For fhelter there the trembling fhadow bent: 925
And fkip'd and fculk'd, and under hatches went.
Exulting Turnus, with regardlefs hafte
Afcends the plank, and to the gally pafs'd:
Scarce had he reach'd the prow, Saturnia's hand
The haulfers cuts, and fhoots the fhip from land.   930

With wind in poop, the veffel ploughs the fea,
And meafures back with fpeed her former way.
Mean time Æneas feeks his abfent foe,
And fends his flaughter'd troops to fhades below.

   The guileful phantom now forfook the fhrowd, 935.
And flew fublime, and vanifh'd in a cloud.
Too late young Turnus the delufion found,
Far on the fea, ftill making from the ground.
Then thanklefs for a life redeem'd by fhame;
With fenfe of honour ftung, and forfeit fame,   940
Fearful befides of what in fight had pafs'd,
His hands, and hagard eyes to heav'n he caft.
O Jove! he cry'd, for what offence have I
Deferv'd to bear this endlefs infamy?
Whence am I forc'd, and whither am I born,   945.
How, and with what reproach fhall I return!
Shall ever I behold the Latian plain,
Or fee Laurentum's lofty tow'rs again?
What will they fay of their deferting chief?
The war was mine, I fly from their relief: 950
I led to flaughter, and in flaughter leave;
And ev'n from hence their dying groans receive.
Here over-match'd in fight, in heaps they lie,
There fcatter'd o'er the fields ignobly fly.   954

Gape wide, O earth! and draw me down alive, ⎫
Or, oh ye pitying winds, a wretch relieve; ⎬
On fands or fhelves the fplitting veffel drive: ⎭
Or fet me fhipwreck'd on fome defart fhore,
Where no Rutulian eyes may fee me more:
Unknown to friends, or foes, or confcious fame, 960
Left fhe fhou'd follow, and my flight proclaim.

 Thus Turnus rav'd, and various fates revolv'd,
The choice was doubtful, but the death refolv'd.
And now the fword, and now the fea took place:
That to revenge, and this to purge difgrace. 965
Sometimes he thought to fwim the ftormy main,
By ftretch of arms the diftant fhore to gain:
Thrice he the fword affay'd, and thrice the flood;
But Juno mov'd with pity both withftood:
And thrice reprefs'd his rage: ftrong gales fupply'd,
And pufh'd the veffel o'er the fwelling tide. 971
At length fhe lands him on his native fhores,
And to his father's longing arms reftores.

 Mean time, by Jove's impulfe, Mezentius arm'd:
Succeeding Turnus, with his ardor warm'd 975
His fainting friends, reproach'd their fhameful flight,
Repell'd the victors, and renew'd the fight.
Againft their king the Tufcan troops confpire,
Such is their hate, and fuch their fierce defire

Of wish'd revenge : on him, and him alone,   980
All hands employ'd, and all their darts are thrown.
He, like a solid rock by seas inclos'd,
To raging winds and roaring waves oppos'd ;
From his proud summit looking down, disdains
Their empty menace, and unmov'd remains.   985
    Beneath his feet fell haughty Hebrus dead,
Then Latagus ; and Palmus as he fled :
At Latagus a weighty stone he flung,
His face was flatted, and his helmet rung.
But Palmus from behind receives his wound,   990
Hamstring'd he falls, and grovels on the ground :
His crest and armour from his body torn,
Thy shoulders, Lausus, and thy head adorn.
Evas and Mymas, both of Troy, he slew,
Mymas his birth from fair Theano drew :   995
Born on that fatal night, when, big with fire,
The queen produc'd young Paris to his sire.
But Paris in the Phrygian fields was slain,
Unthinking Mymus on the Latian plain.
    And, as a savage boar on mountains bred,   1000
With forest mast, and fatning marshes fed ;
When once he sees himself in toils inclos'd,
By huntsmen and their eager hounds oppos'd :

He whets his tufks, and turns, and dares the war:
Th' invaders dart their jav'lins from afar;　　1005
All keep aloof, and fafely fhout around,
But none prefumes to give a nearer wound.
He frets and froths, erects his briftled hide,
And fhakes a grove of lances from his fide:
Not otherwife the troops, with hate infpir'd　　1010
And juft revenge, againft the tyrant fir'd;
Their darts with clamour at a diftance drive:
And only keep the languifh'd war alive.

　　From Coritus came Acron to the fight,
Who left his fpoufe betroth'd, and unconfummate
　　　　　　　　　　　　　　　　　　[night.
Mezentius fees him thro' the fquadrons ride,　　1016
Proud of the purple favours of his bride.
Then, as a hungry lion, who beholds
A gamefom goat, who frifks about the folds:
Or beamy ftag that grazes on the plain:　　1020
He runs, he roars, he fhakes his rifing mane;
He grins, and opens wide his greedy jaws,
The prey lies panting underneath his paws;
He fills his famifh'd maw, his mouth runs o'er
With unchew'd morfels, while he churns the gore:
So proud Mezentius rufhes on his foes,　　1026
And firft unhappy Acron overthrows:

Stretch'd at his length, he spurns the swarthy ground,

The lance besmear'd with blood, lies broken in the
[wound.

Then with disdain the haughty victor view'd 1030

Orodes flying, nor the wretch pursu'd :

Nor thought the dastard's back deserv'd a wound,

But running gain'd th' advantage of the ground.

Then turning short, he met him face to face,

To give his victory the better grace. 1035

Orodes falls, in equal fight oppress'd :

Mezentius fix'd his foot upon his breast,

And rested lance : and thus aloud he cries,

Lo here the champion of my rebels lies.

The fields around with Iö Pæan ring, 1040

And peals of shouts applaud the conqu'ring king.

At this the vanquish'd, with his dying breath,

Thus faintly spoke, and prophesy'd in death :

Nor thou, proud man, unpunish'd shalt remain ;

Like death attends thee on this fatal plain. 1045

Then, sourly smiling, thus the king reply'd,

For what belongs to me, let Jove provide :

But die thou first, whatever chance ensue :

He said, and from the wound the weapon drew :

A hov'ring mist came swimming o'er his sight, 1050

And seal'd his eyes in everlasting night.

By Cadicus, Alcathous was flain;
Sacrator laid Hydafpes on the plain:
Orfes the ftrong to greater ftrength muft yield:
He, with Parthenius, were by Rapo kill'd.   1055
Then brave Meffapus Ericetes flew,
Who from Lycaon's blood his lineage drew.
But from his headftrong horfe his fate he found, ⎱
Who threw his mafter as he made a bound,   ⎰
The chief alighting, ftuck him to the ground. 1060⎰
Then Clonius hand to hand, on foot affails,
The Trojan finks, and Neptune's fon prevails.

Agis the Lycian ftepping forth with pride,
To fingle fight the boldeft foe defy'd.
Whom Tufcan Valerus by force o'ercame,   1065
And not bely'd his mighty father's fame.
Salius to death the great Antronius fent,
But the fame fate the victor underwent;
Slain by Nealces' hand, well fkill'd to throw 1069
The flying dart, and draw the far-deceiving bow.

Thus equal deaths are dealt with equal chance;
By turns they quit their ground, by turns advance;
Victors, and vanquifh'd in the various field,
Nor wholly overcome, nor wholly yield.

The gods from heav'n furvey the fatal ftrife, 1075
And mourn the miferies of human life.
Above the reft two goddeffes appear
Concern'd for each : here Venus, Juno there :
Amidft the crowd infernal Atè fhakes
Her fcourge aloft, and creft of hiffing fnakes. 1080

Once more the proud Mezentius with difdain,
Brandifh'd his fpear, and rufh'd into the plain :
Where tow'ring in the midmoft ranks he ftood,
Like tall Orion ftalking o'er the flood :
When with his brawny breaft he cuts the waves, 1085
His fhoulders fcarce the topmoft billow laves.
Or like a mountain-afh, whofe roots are fpread,
Deep fix'd in earth, in clouds he hides his head.

The Trojan prince beheld him from afar,
And dauntlefs undertook the doubtful war.   1090
Collected in his ftrength, and like a rock,
Poiz'd on his bafe, Mezentius ftood the fhock.
He ftood, and meafuring firft with careful eyes,
The fpace his fpear cou'd reach, aloud he cries ;
My ftrong right hand, and fword, affift my ftroke ;
(Thofe only, gods, Mezentius will invoke) 1096
His armour from the Trojan pirate torn,
By my triumphant Laufus fhall be worn.

He faid, and with his utmoft force he threw
The maffy fpear, which, hiffing as it flew,   1100
Reach'd the celeftial fhield that ftop'd the courfe;
But glancing thence, the yet-unbroken force
Took a new bent obliquely, and betwixt
The fide and bowels fam'd Anthores fix'd.
Anthores had from Argos travell'd far,   1105
Alcides' friend, and brother of the war :
Till tir'd with toils, fair Italy he chofe,
And in Evander's palace fought repofe :
Now falling by another wound, his eyes
He cafts to heav'n, on Argos thinks, and dies.   1110
    The pious Trojan then his jav'lin fent,
The fhield gave way : thro' treble plates it went
Of folid brafs, of linen trebly roll'd,
And three bull-hides which round the buckler roll'd
All thefe it pafs'd, refiftlefs in the courfe,   1115
Tranfpierc'd his thigh, and fpent its dying force.
The gaping wound gufh'd out a crimfon flood;
The Trojan, glad with fight of hoftile blood,
His fauchion drew, to clofer fight addrefs'd,
And with new force his fainting foe opprefs'd.   1120
    His father's peril Laufus view'd with grief,
He figh'd, he wept, he ran to his relief.

And here, heroick youth, 'tis here I muſt
To thy immortal memory be juſt;
And ſing an act ſo noble and ſo new,   1125
Poſterity will ſcarce believe 'tis true.
Pain'd with his wound, and uſeleſs for the fight,
The father ſought to ſave himſelf by flight:
Incumber'd, ſlow he drag'd the ſpear along,   1129
Which pierc'd his thigh, and in his buckler hung.
The pious youth, reſolv'd on death below
The lifted ſword, ſprings forth to face the foe;
Protects his parent, and prevents the blow.
Shouts of applauſe ran ringing thro' the field,
To ſee the ſon the vanquiſh'd father ſhield: 1135
All fir'd with gen'rous indignation ſtrive;
And with a ſtorm of darts, at diſtance drive
The Trojan chief: who held at bay from far,
On his vulcanian orb ſuſtain'd the war.

    As when thick hail comes rattling in the wind, 1140
The ploughman, paſſenger, and lab'ring hind
For ſhelter to the neighb'ring covert fly;
Or, hous'd, or ſafe in hollow caverns lie:
But that o'erblown, when heav'n above 'em ſmiles,
Return to travel, and renew their toils: 1145

Æneas thus o'erwhelm'd on ev'ry fide,
The ftorm of darts, undaunted, did abide;
And thus to Laufus loud with friendly threatning
[cry'd.

Why wilt thou rufh to certain death, and rage
In rafh attempts, beyond thy tender age,   1150
Betray'd by pious love? Nor thus forborn
The youth defifts, but with infulting fcorn
Provokes the ling'ring prince: whofe patience tir'd,
Gave place, and all his breaft with fury fir'd.
For now the fates prepar'd their fharpen'd fheers;
And lifted high the flaming fword appears.   1156
Which full defcending, with a frightful fway,
Thro' fhield and corflet forc'd th' impetuous way,
And buried deep in his fair bofom lay.
The purple ftreams thro' the thin armour ftrove, 1160
And drench'd th' embroider'd coat his mother wove:
And life at length forfook his heaving heart,
Loth from fo fweet a manfion to depart.

But when, with blood, and palenefs all o'erfpread,
The pious prince beheld young Laufus dead;   1165
He griev'd, he wept, the fight an image brought
Of his own filial love; a fadly pleafing thought.

F 3

Then ftretch'd his hand to hold him up, and faid,
Poor haplefs youth ! what praifes can be paid
To love fo great, to fuch tranfcendent ftore   1170
Of early worth, and fure prefage of more !
Accept whate'er Æneas can afford,
Untouch'd thy arms, untaken be thy fword :
And all that pleas'd thee living, ftill remain
Inviolate, and facred to the flain.   1175
Thy body on thy parents I beftow,
To reft thy foul, at leaft if fhadows know,
Or have a fenfe of human things below.
There to thy fellow-ghofts with glory tell,
'Twas by the great Æneas' hand I fell.   1180
With this his diftant friends he beckons near,
Provokes their duty, and prevents their fear :
Himfelf affifts to lift him from the ground,
With clotted locks, and blood that well'd from out
                                    [the wound.

Mean time his father, now no father, ftood,   1185
And wafh'd his wounds by Tiber's yellow flood :
Opprefs'd with anguifh, panting, and o'erfpent,
His fainting limbs againft an oak he leant.
A bough his brazen helmet did fuftain,
His heavier arms lay fcatter'd on the plain :   1190

A chofen train of youth around him ftand,
His drooping head was refted on his hand:
His grifly beard his penfive bofom fought,
And all on Laufus ràn his reftlefs thought.
Careful, concern'd his danger to prevent, 1195
He much enquir'd, and many a meffage fent
To warn him from the field: alas! in vain;
Behold his mournful followers bear him flain:
O'er his broad fhield ftill gufh'd the yawning wound,
And drew a bloody trail along the ground. 1200

 Far off he heard their cries, far off divin'd
The dire event with a foreboding mind.
With duft he fprinkled firft his hoary head,
Then both his lifted hands to heav'n he fpread;
Laft the dear corps embracing, thus he faid. 1205
What joys, alas! cou'd this frail being give,
That I have been fo covetous to live?
To fee my fon, and fuch a fon, refign
His life a ranfom for preferving mine?
And am I then preferv'd, and art thou loft? 1210
How much too dear has that redemption coft!
'Tis now my bitter banifhment I feel;
This is a wound too deep for time to heal.

F 4.

My guilt thy growing virtues did defame,
My blacknefs blotted thy unblemifh'd name.   1215
Chas'd from a throne, abandon'd, and exil'd
For foul mifdeeds, were punifhments too mild :
I ow'd my people thefe, and from their hate,
With lefs refentment cou'd have born my fate.
And yet I live, and yet fuftain the fight   1220
Of hated men, and of more hated light :
But will not long. With that he rais'd from ground
His fainting limbs that ftagger'd with his wound.
Yet with a mind refolv'd, and unappal'd
With pains or perils, for his courfer call'd :   1225
Well-mouth'd, well-manag'd, whom himfelf did⎤
                                             [drefs, ⎮
With daily care, and mounted with fuccefs;   ⎬
His aid in arms, his ornament in peace.   ⎦

  Soothing his courage with a gentle ftroke,
The fteed feem'd fenfible, while thus he fpoke.   1230
O Rhæbus, we have liv'd too long for me,
(If life and long were terms that cou'd agree)
This day thou either fhalt bring back the head,
And bloody trophies of the Trojan dead :
This day thou either fhalt revenge my woe   1235
For murder'd Laufus, on his cruel foe;

Or if inexorable Fate deny
Our conqueſt, with thy conquer'd maſter die :
For after ſuch a lord, I reſt ſecure,   1239
Thou wilt no foreign reins, or Trojan load endure.
He ſaid : and ſtraight th' officious courſer kneels
To take his wonted weight.   His hands he fills
With pointed jav'lins : on his head he lac'd
His glitt'ring helm, which terribly was grac'd
With waving horſe-hair, nodding from afar;   1245
Then ſpurr'd his thund'ring ſteed amidſt the war.
Love, anguiſh, wrath, and grief, to madneſs wrought,
Deſpair, and ſecret ſhame, and conſcious thought
Of inborn worth, his lab'ring ſoul oppreſs'd,
Roll'd in his eyes, and rag'd within his breaſt. 1250
Then loud he call'd Æneas thrice by name,
The loud repeated voice to glad Æneas came.
Great Jove, he ſaid, and the far-ſhooting god,
Inſpire thy mind to make thy challenge good.
He ſpoke no more, but haſten'd, void of fear,   1255
And threaten'd with his long protended ſpear.

    To whom Mezentius thus. Thy vaunts are vain,
My Lauſus lies extended on the plain :
He's loſt ! thy conqueſt is already won,
The wretched ſire is murder'd in the ſon.   1260

F. 5

Nor fate I fear, but all the gods defy,
Forbear thy threats, my bus'nefs is to die;
But firſt receive this parting legacy.
He ſaid: and ſtraight a whirling dart he ſent:
Another after, and another went.   1265
Round in a ſpacious ring he rides the field,
And vainly plies th' impenetrable ſhield:
Thrice rode he round, and thrice Æneas wheel'd,
Turn'd as he turn'd; the golden orb withſtood
The ſtrokes; and bore about an iron wood.   1270
Impatient of delay, and weary grown,
Still to defend, and to defend alone:
To wrench the darts which in his buckler light,
Urg'd, and o'er-labour'd in unequal fight:
At length refolv'd, he throws with all his force, 1275
Full at the temples of the warrior horſe.
Juſt where the ſtroke was aim'd, th' unerring ſpear
Made way, and ſtood transfix'd thro' either ear.
Seiz'd with unwonted pain, ſurpriz'd with fright,
The wonted ſteed curvets; and, rais'd upright, 1280
Lights on his feet before: his hoofs behind
Spring up in air aloft, and laſh the wind.
Down comes the rider headlong from his height,
His horſe came after with unwieldy weight

J. Collver sculp.

And flound'ring forward, pitching on his head, 1285,
His lord's incumber'd fhoulder overlaid.

From either hoft the mingled fhouts, and cries,
Of Trojans and Rutulians rend the fkies:
Æneas haft'ning, wav'd his fatal fword.
High o'er his head, with this reproachful word, 1290
Now, where are now thy vaunts, the fierce difdain
Of proud Mezentius, and the lofty ftrain?

Struggling, and wildly ftaring on the fkies,
With fcarce recover'd fight, he thus replies.
Why thefe infulting words, this wafte of breath,
To fouls undaunted, and fecure of death.   1296
'Tis no difhonour for the brave to die,
Nor came I here with hope of victory:
Nor afk I life, nor fought with that defign:
As I had us'd my fortune, ufe thou thine.   1300
My dying fon contracted no fuch band;
The gift is hateful from his murd'rer's hand.
For this, this only favour let me fue,
If pity can to conquer'd foes be due;
Refufe it not: but let my body have   1305
The laft retreat of human kind, a grave.
Too well I know th' infulting people's hate;
Protect me from their vengeance after fate:

F 6

This refuge for my poor remains provide,
And lay my much-lov'd Laufus by my fide: 1310
He faid, and to the fword his throat apply'd.
The crimfon ftream diftain'd his arms around,
And the difdainful foul came rufhing thro' the
[wound.

THE

ELEVENTH BOOK

OF THE

ÆNEIS.

THE

ARGUMENT.

Æ NE AS erects a trophy of the spoils of Mezen-
tius; grants a truce for burying the dead; and
sends home the body of Pallas with great solemnity.
Latinus calls a council to propose offers of peace to
Æneas, which occasions great animosity betwixt Turnus
and Drances: in the mean time there is a sharp en-
gagement of the horse; wherein Camilla signalizes her-
self; is kill'd: and the Latine troops are intirely
defeated.

The Eleventh Book of the

Æ N E I S.

SCARCE had the rofy morning rais'd her head
  Above the waves, and left her wat'ry bed;
The pious chief whom double cares attend
For his unbury'd foldiers, and his friend:
Yet firft to heav'n perform'd a victor's vows: 5
He bar'd an ancient oak of all her boughs:
Then on a rifing ground the trunk he plac'd;
Which with the fpoils of his dead foe he grac'd.
The coat of arms by proud Mezentius worn,
Now on a naked fhag in triumph born,   10
Was hung on high; and glitter'd from afar:
A trophy facred to the god of war.
Above his arms, fix'd on the leaflefs wood,
Appear'd his plumy creft, befmear'd with blood;

His brazen buckler on the left was feen;   15
Truncheons of fhiver'd lances hung between :
And on the right was plac'd his corflet, bor'd ;
And to the neck was ty'd his unavailing fword.
A crowd of chiefs inclofe the godlike man :
Who thus, confpicuous in the midft, began.   20
Our toils, my friends, are crown'd with fure fuccefs :
The greater part perform'd, atchieve the lefs.
Now follow chearful to the trembling town ;
Prefs but an entrance, and prefume it won.
Fear is no more : for fierce Mezentius lies,   25
As the firft fruits of war, a facrifice.
Turnus fhall fall extended on the plain ;
And in this omen is already flain.
Prepar'd in arms, purfue your happy chance :
That none unwarn'd, may plead his ignorance :   30
And I, at heav'n's appointed hour, may find
Your warlike enfigns waving in the wind.
Mean time the rites and fun'ral pomps prepare,
Due to your dead companions of the war :
The laft refpect the living can beftow,   35
To fhield their fhadows from contempt below.
That conquer'd earth be theirs for which they fought;
And which for us with their own blood they bought.

But firft the corps of our unhappy friend,
To the fad city of Evander fend :   40
Who not inglorious in his age's bloom,
Was hurry'd hence by too fevere a doom.

   Thus, weeping while he fpoke, he took his way,
Where, new in death, lamented Pallas lay :
Accœtes watch'd the corps; whofe youth deferv'd 45
The father's truft, and now the fon he ferv'd
With equal faith, but lefs aufpicious care :
Th' attendants of the flain his forrow fhare.
A troop of Trojans mix'd with thefe appear,
And mourning matrons with difhevell'd hair.   50
Soon as the prince appears, they raife a cry;
All beat their breafts, and echoes rend the fky.
They rear his drooping forehead from the ground;
But when Æneas view'd the grifly wound
Which Pallas in his manly bofom bore,   55
And the fair flefh diftain'd with purple gore :
Firft, melting into tears, the pious man
Deplor'd fo fad a fight, then thus began.

   Unhappy youth ! when fortune gave the reft
Of my full wifhes, fhe refus'd the beft !   60
She came ; but brought not thee along, to blefs
My longing eyes, and fhare in my fuccefs :

She grudg'd thy safe return, the triumphs due
To prosp'rous valour, in the publick view.
Not thus I promis'd, when my father lent   65
Thy needless succour with a sad consent;
Embrac'd me parting for th' Etrurian land,
And sent me to possess a large command.
He warn'd, and from his own experience told,
Our foes were warlike, disciplin'd, and bold: 70
And now perhaps, in hopes of thy return,
Rich odours on his loaded altars burn;
While we, with vain officious pomp, prepare
To send him back his portion of the war;
A bloody breathless body: which can owe   75
No farther debt, but to the pow'rs below.
The wretched father, ere his race is run,
Shall view the fun'ral honours of his son.
These are my triumphs of the Latian-war;
Fruits of my plighted faith, and boasted care.   80
And yet, unhappy sire, thou shalt not see
A son, whose death disgrac'd his ancestry;
Thou shalt not blush, old man, however griev'd:
Thy Pallas no dishonest wound receiv'd.
He dy'd no death to make thee wish, too late,   85
Thou hadst not liv'd to see his shameful fate.

But what a champion has th' Aufonian coaft,
And what a friend haft thou, Afcanius, loft!

  Thus having mourn'd, he gave the word around,
To raife the breathlefs body from the ground;   90
And chofe a thoufand horfe, the flow'r of all
His warlike troops, to wait the funeral:
To bear him back, and fhare Evander's grief;
(A well-becoming, but a weak relief.)
Of oaken twigs they twift an eafy bier;   95
Then on their fhoulders the fad burden rear.
The body on this rural herfe is born,
Strew'd leaves and fun'ral greens the bier adorn.
All pale he lies, and looks a lovely flow'r,
New cropt by virgin hands, to drefs the bow'r: 100
Unfaded yet, but yet unfed below,
No more to mother earth or the green ftem fhall owe.
Then two fair vefts, of wond'rous work and coft,
Of purple woven, and with gold embofs'd,
For ornament the Trojan hero brought,   105
Which with her hands Sidonian Dido wrought.
One veft array'd the corps, and one they fpread
O'er his clos'd eyes, and wrap'd around his head:
That when the yellow hair in flame fhou'd fall,
The catching fire might burn the golden caul. 110

Befides, the fpoils of foes in battle flain,
When he defcended on the Latian plain:
Arms, trappings, horfes, by the herfe he led
In long array, (th' atchievements of the dead.)
Then, pinion'd with their hands behind, appear 115
Th' unhappy captives, marching in the rear:
Appointed off'rings in the victor's name,
To fprinkle with their blood, the fun'ral flame.
Inferior trophies by the chiefs are born;
Gantlets and helms, their loaded hands adorn;   120
And fair infcription's fix'd, and titles read
Of Latian leaders conquer'd by the dead.

    Acœtes on his pupil's corps attends,
With feeble fteps; fupported by his friends:
Paufing at ev'ry pace, in forrow drown'd,   125
Betwixt their arms he finks upon the ground.
Where grov'ling, while he lies in deep defpair,
He beats his breaft, and rends his hoary hair.
The champion's chariot next is feen to roll,
Befmear'd with hoftile blood, and honourably foul.
To clofe the pomp, Æthon, the fteed of ftate,   131
Is led, the fun'rals of his lord to wait.
Stripp'd of his trappings, with a fullen pace
He walks, and the big tears run rolling down his face.

The lance of Pallas, and the crimſon creſt,   135
Are born behind ; the victor ſeiz'd the reſt.
The march begins: The trumpets hoarſly ſound,
The pikes and lances trail along the ground.
Thus while the Trojan and Arcadian horſe,
To Pallantean tow'rs direct their courſe,   140
In long proceſſion rank'd ; the pious chief
Stop'd in the rear, and gave a vent to grief.
The publick care, he ſaid, which war attends,
Diverts our preſent woes, at leaſt ſuſpends :
Peace with the manes of great Pallas dwell ;   145
Hail holy relicks, and a laſt farewell !
He ſaid no more, but inly though he mourn'd,
Reſtrain'd his tears, and to the camp return'd.
    Now ſuppliants, from Laurentum ſent, demand
A truce, with olive branches in their hand.   150
Obteſt his clemency, and from the plain
Beg leave to draw the bodies of their ſlain.
They plead, that none thoſe common rites deny
To conquer'd foes, that in fair battle die.
All cauſe of hate was ended in their death ;   155
Nor cou'd he war with bodies void of breath.
A king, they hop'd, would hear a king's requeſt:
Whoſe ſon he once was call'd, and once his gueſt.

Their fuit, which was too juft to be deny'd,
The hero grants, and farther thus reply'd :   160
O Latian princes, how fevere a fate
In caufelefs quarrels has involv'd your ftate !
And arm'd againft an unoffending man,
Who fought your friendfhip ere the war began !
You beg a truce, which I would gladly give,   165
Not only for the flain, but thofe who live.
I came not hither but by heav'n's command,
And fent by fate to fhare the Latian land.
Nor wage I wars unjuft; your king deny'd
My proffer'd friendfhip, and my promis'd bride.   170
Left me for Turnus; Turnus then fhould try
His caufe in arms, to conquer or to die.
My right and his are in difpute : the flain
Fell without fault, our quarrel to maintain.
In equal arms let us alone contend ;   175
And let him vanquifh, whom his fates befriend.
This is the way, fo tell him, to poffefs
The royal virgin, and reftore the peace.
Bear this my meffage back ; with ample leave
That your flain friends may fun'ral rites receive. 180
   Thus having faid, th' embaffadors amaz'd,
Stood mute a while, and on each other gaz'd :

Drances, their chief, who harbour'd in his breaſt
Long hate to Turnus, as his foe profeſs'd,
Broke ſilence firſt, and to the godlike man,   185
With graceful action bowing, thus began.

   Aufpicious prince, in arms a mighty name,
But yet whoſe actions far tranſcend your fame:
Wou'd I your juſtice or your force expreſs,
Thought can but equal; and all words are leſs: 190
Your anſwer we ſhall thankfully relate,
And favours granted to the Latian ſtate:
If wiſh'd ſucceſs our labour ſhall attend,
Think peace concluded, and the king your friend:
Let Turnus leave the realm to your command: 195
And ſeek alliance in ſome other land:
Build you the city which your fates aſſign:
We ſhall be proud in the great work to join.
  Thus Drances; and his words ſo well perſuade
The reſt impower'd, that ſoon a truce is made. 200
Twelve days the term allow'd: and during thoſe,
Latians and Trojans, now no longer foes,
Mix'd in the woods, for fun'ral piles prepare,
To fell the timber, and forget the war.
Loud axes thro' the groning groves refound: 205
Oak, mountain-aſh, and poplar, ſpread the ground:

Firs fall from high: and fome the trunks receive,
In loaden wains, with wedges fome they cleave.

. And now the fatal news, by Fame is blown
Thro' the fhort circuit of th' Arcadian town,   210
Of Pallas flain: by Fame, which juft before
His triumphs on diftended pinions bore.
Rufhing from out the gate, the people ftand,
Each with a fun'ral flambeau in his hand:
Wildly they ftare, diftracted with amaze: 215
The fields are lighten'd with a fiery blaze,
That caft a fullen fplendor on their friends,
(The marching troop which their dread prince at-
                                    [tends.)

Both parties meet: they raife a doleful cry:
The matrons from the walls with fhrieks reply: 220
And their mix'd mourning rends the vaulted fky.
The town is fill'd with tumult and with tears,
Till the loud clamours reach Evander's ears:
Forgetful of his ftate, he runs along,
With a diforder'd pace, and cleaves the throng: 225
Falls on the corps, and groaning there he lies,
With filent grief, that fpeaks but at his eyes:
Short fighs and fobs fucceed: till forrow breaks
A paffage, and at once he weeps and fpeaks.

O Pallas! thou haſt fail'd thy plighted word! 230
To fight with caution, not to tempt the ſword,
I warn'd thee, but in vain; for well I knew
What perils youthful ardour would purſue:
That boiling blood would carry thee too far;
Young as thou wert in dangers, raw to war!   235
O curſt eſſay of arms, diſaſtrous doom,
Prelude of bloody fields, and fights to come!
Hard elements of inauſpicious war,
Vain vows to heav'n, and unavailing care!
Thrice happy thou, dear partner of my bed,   240
Whoſe holy ſoul the ſtroke of fortune fled:
Præſcious of ills, and leaving me behind,
To drink the dregs of life by fate aſſign'd.
Beyond the goal of nature I have gone;
My Pallas late ſet out but reach'd too ſoon.   245
If, from my league againſt th' Auſonian ſtate,
Amidſt their weapons I had found my fate,
(Deſerv'd from them) then I had been return'd
A breathleſs victor, and my ſon had mourn'd.
Yet will not I my Trojan friend upbraid,   250
Nor grudge th' alliance I ſo gladly made.
'Twas not his fault my Pallas fell ſo young,
But my own crime for having liv'd too long.

Vol. IV.   G

Yet, since the gods had destin'd him to die,
At least he led the way to victory :   255
First for his friends he won the fatal shore,
And sent whole herds of slaughter'd foes before:
A death too great, too glorious to deplore.
Nor will I add new honours to thy grave ;
Content with those the Trojan hero gave.   260
That fun'ral pomp thy Phrygian friends design'd;
In which the Tuscan chiefs, and army join'd :
Great spoils, and trophies gain'd by thee, they bear:
Then let thy own atchievements be thy share.
Ev'n thou, O Turnus, hadst a trophy stood,   265
Whose mighty trunk had better grac'd the wood.
If Pallas had arriv'd, with equal length
Of years, to match thy bulk with equal strength.
But why, unhappy man, dost thou detain
These troops to view the tears thou shed'st in vain!
Go, friends, this message to your lord relate;   271
Tell him, that if I bear my bitter fate,
And after Pallas' death, live ling'ring on,
'Tis to behold his vengeance for my son.
I stay for Turnus; whose devoted head   275
Is owing to the living and the dead :
My son and I expect it from his hand;
'Tis all that he can give, or we demand.

Joy is no more : but I would gladly go,
To greet my Pallas with fuch news below.   280·
   The morn had now difpell'd the fhades of night;
Reftoring toils, when fhe reftor'd the light :
The Trojan king, and Tufcan chief, command
To raife the piles along the winding ftrand :   284
Their friends convey the dead to fun'ral fires ;   ⎫
Black fmouldring fmoke from the green wood ex- ⎪
                                  [pires ; ⎬
The light of heav'n is chok'd, and the new day ⎪
                                  [retires. ⎭
Then thrice around the kindled piles they go :
(For ancient cuftom had ordain'd it fo)
Thrice horfe and foot about the fires are led,   290
And thrice with loud laments they hail the dead.
Tears trickling down their breafts bedew the ground ;
And drums and trumpets mix their mournful found.
Amid the blaze, their pious brethren throw
The fpoils, in battle taken from the foe ;   295
Helms, bitts embofs'd, and fwords of fhining fteel,
One cafts a target, one a chariot-wheel :
Some to their fellows their own arms reftore :
The fauchions which in lucklefs fight they bore :
                     G 2

Their bucklers pierc'd, their darts beftow'd in vain,
And fhiver'd lances gather'd from the plain,   301
Whole herds of offer'd bulls about the fire,
And briftled boars, and woolly fheep expire.
Around the piles a careful troop attends,
To watch the wafting flames, and weep their burn-
                                    [ing friends.
Ling'ring along the fhore, till dewy night   306
New decks the face of heav'n with ftarry light.

   The conquer'd Latians, with like pious care,
Piles without number for their dead prepare;
Part, in the places where they fell, are laid;   310
And part are to the neighb'ring fields convey'd.
The corps of kings, and captains of renown,
Born off in ftate, are bury'd in the town:
The reft unhonour'd, and without a name,
Are caft a common heap to feed the flame.   315
Trojans and Latians vie with like defires
To make the field of battle fhine with fires;
And the promifcuous blaze to heav'n afpires.

   Now had the morning thrice renew'd the light,
And thrice difpell'd the fhadows of the night;   320
When thofe who round the wafted fires remain,
Perform the laft fad office to the flain:

They rake the yet warm afhes, from below;
Thefe, and the bones unburn'd, in earth beftow:
Thefe relicks with their country rites they grace;
And raife a mount of turf to mark the place.   326

  But in the palace of the king, appears
A fcene more folemn, and a pomp of tears.
Maids, matrons, widows, mix their common moans:
Orphans their fires, and fires lament their fons.   330
All' in that univerfal forrow fhare;
And curfe the caufe of this unhappy war.
A broken league, a bride unjuftly fought,
A crown ufurp'd, which with their blood is bought!
Thefe are the crimes, with which they load the name
Of Turnus, and on him alone exclaim.   336
Let him, who lords it o'er th' Aufonian land,
Engage the Trojan hero hand to hand:
His is the gain, our lot is but to ferve:
'Tis juft, the fway he feeks, he fhould deferve.   340
This Drances aggravates; and adds, with fpight,
His foe expects, and dares him to the fight.
Nor Turnus wants a party, to fupport
His caufe and credit, in the Latian court.
His former acts fecure his prefent fame;   345
And the queen fhades him with her mighty name.

While thus their factious minds with fury burn;
The legates from th' Ætolian prince return:
Sad news they bring, that after all the cost,
And care employ'd, their embassy is lost: 350
That Diomede refus'd his aid in war;
Unmov'd with presents, and as deaf to pray'r.
Some new alliance must elsewhere be sought;
Or peace with Troy on hard conditions bought.

Latinus, sunk in sorrow, finds too late   355
A foreign son is pointed out by fate:
And till Æneas shall Lavinia wed,
The wrath of heav'n is hov'ring o'er his head.
The gods, he saw, espous'd the juster side,
When late their titles in the field were try'd: 360
Witness the fresh laments, and fun'ral tears un-
[dry'd.

Thus, full of anxious thought, he summons all
The Latian senate to the council hall:
The princes come, commanded by their head,
And crowd the paths that to the palace lead.   365
Supreme in pow'r, and reverenc'd for his years,
He takes the throne, and in the midst appears:
Majestically sad, he sits in state,
And bids his envoys their success relate.

When Venulus began, the murmuring found 370
Was hufh'd, and facred filence reign'd around.
We have, faid he, perform'd your high command:
And pafs'd with peril a long tract of land :
We reach'd the place defir'd, with wonder fill'd,
The Grecian tents, and rifing tow'rs beheld.   375
Great Diomede has compafs'd round with walls
The city, which Argyripa he calls ;
From his own Argos nam'd : we touch'd, with joy,
The royal hand that raz'd unhappy Troy.
When introduc'd, our prefents firft we bring,   380
Then crave an inftant audience from the king:
His leave obtain'd, our native foil we name ;
And tell th' important caufe for which we came.
Attentively he heard us, while we fpoke ;
Then, with foft accents, and a pleafing look,   385
Made this return. Aufonian race of old
Renown'd for peace, and for an age of gold,
What madnefs has your alter'd minds poffefs'd,
To change for war hereditary reft ?
Solicit arms unknown, and tempt the fword,   390
(A needlefs ill your anceftors abhor'd.)
We, (for myfelf I fpeak, and all the name
Of Grecians, who to Troy's deftruction came ;)

Omitting thofe who were in battle flain,
Or born by rolling Simois to the main :   395
Not one but fuffer'd, and too dearly bought
The prize of honour which in arms he fought.
Some doom'd to death, and fome in exile driv'n,
Out-cafts, abandon'd by the care of heav'n :
So worn, fo wretched, fo defpis'd a crew,   400
As ev'n old Priam might with pity view.
Witnefs the veffels by Minerva tofs'd
In ftorms, the vengeful Caphaærean coaft ;
The Eubæan rocks : the prince, whofe brother led
Our armies to revenge his injur'd bed,   405
In Egypt loft ; Ulyffes, with his men,
Have feen Charybdis, and the Cyclops den :
Why fhould I name Idomeneus, in vain,
Reftor'd to fceptres, and expell'd again ?
Or young Achilles, by his rival flain ?   410
Ev'n he, the king of men, the foremoft name
Of all the Greeks, and moft renown'd by fame,
The proud revenger of another's wife,
Yet by his own adult'refs loft his life :
Fell at his threfhold, and the fpoils of Troy   415
The foul polluters of his bed enjoy.
The gods have envy'd me the fweets of life,
My much-lov'd country, and my more-lov'd wife :

Banish'd from both, I mourn ; while in the sky,
Transform'd to birds, my lost companions fly: 420
Hov'ring about the coasts they make their moan ;
And cuff the cliffs with pinions not their own.
What squalid spectres, in the dead of night,
Break my short sleep, and skim before my sight!
I might have promis'd to myself those harms, 425
Mad as I was, when I with mortal arms
Presum'd against immortal pow'rs to move,
And violate with wounds the queen of love.
Such arms this hand shall never more employ ;
No hate remains with me to ruin'd Troy.   430
I war not with its dust ; nor am I glad
To think of past events, or good or bad.
Your presents I return : whate'er you bring
To buy my friendship, send the Trojan king.
We met in fight, I know him to my cost ;   435
With what a whirling force his lance he tofs'd :
Heav'ns what a spring was in his arm, to throw !
How high he held his shield, and rose at ev'ry blow !
Had Troy produc'd two more, his match in might,
They would have chang'd the fortune of the fight : 440
Th' invasion of the Greeks had been return'd :
Our empire wasted, and our cities burn'd.

The long defence the Trojan people made,
The war protracted, and the fiege delay'd,
Were due to Hector's and this hero's hand;   445
Both brave alike, and equal in command:
Æneas not inferior in the field,
In pious rev'rence to the gods excell'd.
Make peace, ye Latians, and avoid with care
Th' impending dangers of a fatal war.   450
He faid no more; but with this cold excufe,
Refus'd th' alliance, and advis'd a truce.

  Thus Venulus concluded his report.
A jarring murmur fill'd the factious court:
As when a torrent rolls with rapid force,   455
And dafhes o'er the ftones that ftop the courfe;
The flood, conftrain'd within a fcanty fpace,
Roars horrible along th' uneafy race:
White foam in gath'ring eddies floats around:
The rocky fhores rebellow to the found.   460

    The murmur ceas'd: then from his lofty throne
The king invok'd the gods, and thus begun.
I wifh, ye Latins, what we now debate
Had been refolv'd before it was too late:
Much better had it been for you and me,   465
Unforc'd by this our laft neceffity,

To have been earlier wife; than now to call
A council, when the foe furrounds the wall.
O citizens! we wage unequal war,
With men, not only heav'n's peculiar care,   470
But heav'ns own race: unconquer'd in the field,
Or conquer'd, yet unknowing how to yield.
What hopes you had in Diomede, lay down:
Our hopes muſt center on ourſelves alone.
Yet thoſe how feeble, and, indeed, how vain;   475
You ſee too well ; nor need my words explain.
Vanquiſh'd without reſource ; laid flat by Fate,
Factions within, a foe without the gate ;
Not but I grant, that all perform'd their parts,
With manly force, and with undaunted hearts: 480
With our united ſtrength the war we wag'd ;
With equal numbers, equal arms engag'd :
You ſee th' event —— Now hear what I propoſe,
To ſave our friends, and ſatisfy our foes :
A tract of land the Latins have poſſeſs'd   485
Along the Tiber, ſtretching to the weſt,
Which now Rutulians and Auruncans till :
And their mix'd cattle graze the fruitful hill ;
Thoſe mountains fill'd with firs, that lower land,
If you conſent, the Trojan ſhall command ;   490

Call'd into part of what is ours; and there,
On terms agreed, the common country fhare.
There let them build, and fettle if they pleafe;
Unlefs they choofe once more to crofs the feas,
In fearch of feats remote of Italy;   495
And from unwelcome inmates fet us free.
Then twice ten gallies let us build with fpeed,
Or twice as many more, if more they need;
Materials are at hand: a well grown wood
Runs equal with the margin of the flood: 500
Let them the number, and the form affign;
The care and coft of all the ftores be mine.
To treat the peace a hundred fenators
Shall be commiffion'd hence with ample pow'rs; 504
With olive crown'd: the prefents they fhall bear,⎫
A purple robe, a royal iv'ry chair;   ⎪
And all the marks of fway that Latian monarchs   ⎬
                              [wear; ⎭
And fums of gold.   Among yourfelves debate
This great affair, and fave the finking ftate.

    Then Drances took the word; who grudg'd long
                              [fince,
The rifing glories of the Daunian prince.   511

Factious and rich, bold at the council board,
But cautious in the field, he fhun'd the fword ;
A clofe caballer, and tongue-valiant lord.
Noble his mother was, and near the throne,   515.
But what his father's parentage, unknown.
He rofe, and took th' advantage of the times,
To load young Turnus with invidious crimes.

Such truths, O king, faid he, your words contain,
As ftrike the fenfe, and all replies are vain,   520
Nor are your loyal fubjects now to feek
What common needs require ; but fear to fpeak.
Let him give leave of fpeech, that haughty man,
Whofe pride this inaufpicious war began :
For whofe ambition (let me dare to fay,   525
Fear fet apart, tho' death is in my way)
The plains of Latium run with blood around ;
So many valiant heroes bite the ground :
Dejected grief in ev'ry face appears ;
A town in mourning, and a land in tears.   530
While he, th' undoubted author of our harms,
The man who menaces the gods with arms,
Yet after all his boafts, forfook the fight,
And fought his fafety in ignoble flight.

Now, beft of kings, fince you propofe to fend 535
Such bounteous prefents to your Trojan friend ;

Add yet a greater at our joint requeſt,
One which he values more than all the reſt;
Give him the fair Lavinia for his bride:
With that alliance let the league be ty'd;   540
And for the bleeding land a laſting peace provide.
Let inſolence no longer awe the throne,
But with a father's right beſtow your own.
For this maligner of the gen'ral good,
If ſtill we fear his force, he muſt be woo'd: 545
His haughty godhead we with prayers implore,
Your ſceptre to releaſe, and our juſt rights reſtore.
O curſed cauſe of all our ills, muſt we
Wage wars unjuſt, and fall in fight for thee!
What right haſt thou to rule the Latian ſtate,   550
And ſend us out to meet our certain fate?
'Tis a deſtructive war: from Turnus' hand
Our peace and publick ſafety we demand.
Let the fair bride to the brave chief remain;
If not, the peace without the pledge is vain.   555
Turnus, I know you think me not your friend,
Nor will I much with your belief contend:
I beg your greatneſs not to give the law
In other realms, but beaten, to withdraw.
Pity your own, or pity our eſtate;   560
Nor twiſt our fortunes with your ſinking fate.

Your int'reſt is the war ſhould never ceaſe ;
But we have felt enough to wiſh the peace :
A land exhauſted to the laſt remains,
Depopulated towns, and driven plains.   565
Yet, if deſire of fame, and thirſt of pow'r,
A beauteous princeſs, with a crown in dow'r,
So fire your mind, in arms aſſert your right ;
And meet your foe, who dares you to the fight.
Mankind, it ſeems, is made for you alone ;   570
We, but the ſlaves who mount you to a throne :
A baſe ignoble crowd, without a name :
Unwept, unworthy of the fun'ral flame :
By duty bound to forfeit each his life,
That Turnus may poſſeſs a royal wife.   575
Permit not, mighty man, ſo mean a crew
Shou'd ſhare ſuch triumphs ; and detain from you
The poſt of honour, your undoubted due :
Rather alone your matchleſs force employ ;
To merit, what alone you muſt enjoy.   580
        Theſe words, ſo full of malice, mix'd with art,
Inflam'd with rage the youthful hero's heart.
Then groaning from the bottom of his breaſt,
He heav'd for wind, and thus his wrath expreſs'd.
You, Drances, never want a ſtream of words,   585
Then, when the publick need requires our ſwords.

First in the council-hall to steer the state;
And ever foremost in a tongue-debate.
While our strong walls secure us from the foe,
Ere yet with blood our ditches overflow: 590
But let the potent orator declaim,
And with the brand of coward blot my name;
Free leave is giv'n him, when his fatal hand ⎫
Has cover'd with more corps the sanguine strand; ⎬
And high as mine his tow'ring trophies stand. 595 ⎭
If any doubt remains who dares the most,
Let us decide it at the Trojans' cost:
And issue both a-breast, where honour calls;
Foes are not far to seek without the walls.
Unless his noisy tongue can only fight: 600
And feet were giv'n him but to speed his flight.
I beaten from the field? I forc'd away?
Who, but so known a dastard, dares to say?
Had he but ev'n beheld the fight, his eyes
Had witnefs'd for me what his tongue denies: 605
What heaps of Trojans by this hand were slain,
And how the bloody Tiber swell'd the main.
All saw, but he, th' Arcadian troops retire,
In scatter'd squadrons, and their prince expire.
The giant brothers, in their camp, have found, 610
I was not forc'd with ease to quit my ground.

Not fuch the Trojans try'd me, when inclos'd,
I fingly their united arms oppos'd :
Firft forc'd an entrance thro' their thick array; 614
Then, glutted with their flaughter, freed my way.
'Tis a deftructive war ? So let it be,
But to the Phrygian pirate and to thee.
Mean time proceed to fill the people's ears
With falfe reports, their minds with panick fears :
Extol the ftrength of a twice-conquer'd race, 620
Our foes encourage, and our friends debafe.
Believe thy fables, and the Trojan town
Triumphant ftands, the Grecians are o'erthrown :
Suppliant at Hector's feet Achilles lies ;
And Diomede from fierce Æneas flies. 625
Say rapid Aufidus with awful dread,
Runs backward from the fea, and hides his head,
When the great Trojan on his bank appears :
For that's as true as thy diffembled fears
Of my revenge : difmifs that vanity, 630
Thou, Drances, art below a death from me.
Let that vile foul in that vile body reft :
The lodging is well worthy of the gueft.
   Now, royal father, to the prefent ftate
Of our affairs, and of this high debate ; 635

If in your arms thus early you decide,
And think your fortune is already try'd;
If one defeat has brought us down so low;
As never more in fields to meet the foe;
Then I conclude for peace: 'tis time to treat, 640
And lie like vaffals at the victor's feet.
But oh, if any ancient blood remains,
One drop of all our fathers in our veins:
That man wou'd I prefer before the reft,
Who dar'd his death with an undaunted breaft: 645
Who comely fell by no difhoneft wound,
To fhun that fight; and dying gnaw'd the ground.
But if we ftill have frefh recruits in ftore,
If our confed'rates can afford us more;
If the contended field we bravely fought: 650
And not a bloodlefs victory was bought:
Their loffes equal'd ours; and for their flain,
With equal fires they fill'd the fhining plain;
Why thus unforc'd fhou'd we fo tamely yield;
And, ere the trumpet founds, refign the field? 655
Good unexpected, evils unforefeen,
Appear by turns, as Fortune fhifts the fcene:
Some rais'd aloft, come tumbling down amain;
Then fall fo hard, they bound and rife again.

If Diomede refufe his aid to lend,   660

The great Meſſapus yet remains our friend :

Tolumnius, who foretels events, is ours :

Th' Italian chiefs, and princes, join their pow'rs :

Nor leaſt in number, nor in name the laſt,

Your own brave ſubjects have our cauſe embrac'd.665

Above the reſt, the Volſcian Amazon

Contains an army in herſelf alone :

And heads a ſquadron, terrible to fight,

With glitt'ring ſhields, in brazen armour bright.

Yet if the foe a ſingle fight demand,   670

And I alone the publick peace withſtand ;

If you conſent, he ſhall not be refus'd,

Nor find a hand to victory unus'd.

This new Achilles let him take the field,

With fated armour, and Vulcanian ſhield ;   675

For you, my royal father, and my fame,

I, Turnus, not the leaſt of all my name,

Devote my foul.   He calls me hand to hand,

And I alone will anſwer his demand.

Drances ſhall reſt ſecure, and neither ſhare   680

The danger, nor divide the prize of war.

    While they debate ; nor theſe nor thoſe will yield ;

Æneas draws his forces to the field ;

And moves his camp. The fcouts with flying fpeed
Return, and thro' the frighted city fpread   685
Th' unpleafing news, the Trojans are defcry'd
In battle marching by the river's fide;
And bending to the town. They take th' alarm,
Some tremble, fome are bold, all in confufion arm.
Th' impetuous youth prefs forward to the field; 690
They clafh the fword, and clatter on the fhield;
The fearful matrons raife a fcreaming cry;
Old feeble men with fainter groans reply;
A jarring found refults, and mingles in the fky.
Like that of fwans remurm'ring to the floods; 695
Or birds of diff'ring kinds in hollow woods.
Turnus th' occafion takes, and cries aloud,
Talk on, ye quaint haranguers of the crowd:
Declaim in praife of peace, when danger calls;
And the fierce foes in arms approach the walls. 700
He faid, and turning fhort, with fpeedy pace,
Cafts back a fcornful glance, and quits the place.

Thou, Volufus, the Volfcian troops command
To mount; and lead thyfelf our Ardean band.
Meffapus, and Catillus, poft your force   705
Along the fields, to charge the Trojan horfe.
Some guard the paffes, others man the wall;
Drawn up in arms, the reft attend my call.

They fwarm from ev'ry quarter of the town;
And with diforder'd hafte the rampires crown.   710
Good old Latinus, when he faw, too late,
The gath'ring ftorm, juft breaking on the ftate,
Difmifs'd the council, till a fitter time,
And own'd his eafy temper as his crime:
Who, forc'd againft his reafon, had comply'd   715
To break the treaty for the promis'd bride.

   Some help to fink new trenches, others aid
To ram the ftones, or raife the palifade.
Hoarfe trumpets found th' alarm : around the walls
Runs a diftracted crew, whom their laft labour calls.
A fad proceffion in the ftreets is feen,   721
Of matrons that attend the mother-queen:
High in her chair fhe fits, and at her fide,
With down-caft eyes appears the fatal bride.   724
They mount the cliff, where Pallas' temple ftands;
Pray'rs in their mouths, and prefents in their hands;
With cenfers, firft they fume the facred fhrine;
Then in this common fupplication join.
O patronefs of arms, unfpotted maid,
Propitious hear, and lend thy Latins aid: 370
Break fhort the pirate's lance; pronounce his fate,
And lay the Phrygian low before the gate.

Now Turnus arms for fight: his back and breaft,
Well-temper'd fteel, and fcaly brafs inveft:
The cuifhes, which his brawny thighs infold,   735
Are mingled metal damafk'd o'er with gold.
His faithful fauchion fits upon his fide;
Nor cafque, nor creft, his manly features hide:
But bare to view amid furrounding friends,
With godlike grace, he from the tow'r defcends.   740
Exulting in his ftrength, he feems to dare
His abfent rival, and to promife war.
Freed from his keepers, thus with broken reins,
The wanton courfer prances o'er the plains:
Or in the pride of youth o'erleaps the mounds: 745
And fnuffs the females in forbidden grounds.
Or feeks his wat'ring in the well-known flood,
To quench his thirft, and cool his fiery blood:
He fwims luxuriant in the liquid plain,
And o'er his fhoulder flows his waving mane: 750
He neighs, he fnorts, he bears his head on high;
Before his ample cheft the frothy waters fly.
    Soon as the prince appears without the gate,
The Volfcians, and their virgin-leader, wait
His laft commands. Then with a grateful mien,   755
Lights from her lofty fteed, the warrior queen:

Her fquadron imitates, and each defcends;
Whofe common fute Camilla thus commends.
If fenfe of honour, if a foul fecure
Of inborn worth, that can all tefts endure,   760
Can promife ought; or on itfelf rely,
Greatly to dare, to conquer, or to die:
Then, I alone, fuftain'd by thefe, will meet
The Tyrrhene troops, and promife their defeat.
Ours be the danger, ours the fole renown;   765
You, gen'ral, ftay behind, and guard the town.
Turnus a while ftood mute, with glad furprife,
And on the fierce virago fix'd his eyes:
Then thus return'd: O grace of Italy,
With what becoming thanks can I reply!   770
Not only words lie lab'ring in my breaft;
But thought itfelf is by thy praife oppreft;
Yet rob me not of all, but let me join
My toils, my hazard and my fame, with thine.
The Trojan, (not in ftratagem unfkill'd,)   775
Sends his light horfe before to fcour the field:
Himfelf, thro' fteep afcents, and thorny brakes,
A larger compafs to the city takes.
This news my fcouts confirm: and I prepare
To foil his cunning, and his force to dare: 780

With chofen foot his paffage to forelay :
And place an ambufh in the winding way.
Thou, with thy Volfcians, face the Tufcan horfe :
The brave Meffapus fhall thy troops inforce ;
With thofe of Tibur ; and the Latian band :   785
Subjected all to thy fupreme command.

   This faid, he warns Meffapus to the war :
Then ev'ry chief exhorts, with equal care.
All thus encourag'd, his own troops he joins,
And haftes to profecute his deep defigns.   790
Inclos'd with hills, the winding valley lies,
By nature form'd for fraud, and fitted for furprife ;
A narrow track, by human fteps untrode,
Leads, thro' perplexing thorns, to this obfcure abode.
High o'er the vale a fteepy mountain ftands :   795
Whence the furveying fight the nether ground com-
                                [mands.
The top is level : an offenfive feat
Of war ; and from the war a fafe retreat.
For, on the right and left, is room to prefs
The foes at hand, or from afar diftrefs :   800
To drive 'em headlong downward ; and to pour,
On their defcending backs, a ftony fhow'r.
Thither young Turnus took the well-known way ;
Poffefs'd the pafs, and in blind ambufh lay.

Mean time, Latonian Phœbe, from the skies, 805
Beheld th' approaching war with hateful eyes,
And call'd the light-foot Opis to her aid,
Her moſt belov'd, and ever-truſty maid.
Then with a figh began : Camilla goes
To meet her death, amidſt her fatal foes.   810
The nymph I lov'd of all my mortal train ;
Inveſted with Diana's arms, in vain.
Nor is my kindneſs for the virgin, new,
'Twas born with her, and with her years it grew :
Her father Metabus, when forc'd away   815
From old Privernum, for tyrannick ſway ;
Snatch'd up, and ſav'd from his prevailing foes,
This tender babe, companion of his woes.
Caſmilla was her mother ; but he drown'd
One hiſſing letter in a ſofter ſound,   820
And call'd Camilla.   Thro' the woods he flies ;
Wrapt in his robe the royal infant lies.
His foes in fight, he mends his weary pace ;
With ſhouts and clamours they purſue the chace.
The banks of Amaſcene at length he gains ;   825
The raging flood his farther plight reſtrains :
Rais'd o'er the borders with unuſual rains.

Prepar'd to plunge into the ftream, he fears :
Not for himfelf, but for the charge he bears.
Anxious he ftops a while ; and thinks in hafte ; 830
Then, defp'rate in diftrefs, refolves at laft.
A knotty lance of well-boil'd oak he bore ;
The middle part with cork he cover'd o'er :
He clos'd the child within the hollow fpace :
With twigs of bending ofier bound the cafe.   835
Then pois'd the fpear, heavy with human weight :
And thus invok'd my favour for the freight.
Accept, great goddefs of the woods, he faid,
Sent by her fire, this dedicated maid :
Thro' air fhe flies a fuppliant to thy fhrine ;   840
And the firft weapons that fhe knows, are thine.
He faid ; and with full force the fpear he threw ;
Above the founding waves Camilla flew.
Then, prefs'd by foes, he ftemm'd the ftormy tide ;
And gain'd, by ftrefs of arms, the farther fide. 845
His faften'd fpear he pull'd from out the ground ;
And, victor of his vows, his infant nymph unbound.
Nor after that, in towns which walls inclofe,
Wou'd truft his hunted life amidft his foes.
But rough, in open air he chofe to lie :   850
Earth was his couch, his cov'ring was the fky.

On hills unfhorn, or in a defart den,
He fhunn'd the dire fociety of men.
A fhepherd's folitary life he led :
His daughter with the milk of mares he fed ;   855
The dugs of bears, and ev'ry favage beaft,
He drew, and thro' her lips the liquor prefs'd.
The little Amazon cou'd fcarcely go,
He loads her with a quiver and a bow :
And, that fhe might her ftagg'ring fteps command,
He with a flender jav'lin fills her hand :   861
Her flowing hair no golden fillet bound ;
Nor fwept her trailing robe the dufty ground.
Inftead of thefe, a tiger's hide o'erfpread
Her back and fhoulders, faften'd to her head.   865
The flying dart fhe firft attempts to fling ;
And round her tender temples tofs'd the fling :
Then, as her ftrength with years increas'd, began ⎫
To pierce aloft in air the foaring fwan :   ⎬
And from the clouds to fetch the heron and the ⎭
                                    [crane.]
The Tufcan matrons with each other vy'd,   871
To blefs their rival fons with fuch a bride :
But fhe difdains their love ; to fhare with me
The filvan fhades, and vow'd virginity.

H 2

And oh ! I wifh, contented with my cares   875
Of favage fpoils, fhe had not fought the wars :
Then had fhe been of my celeftial train ;
And fhunn'd the fate that dooms her to be flain.
But fince, oppofing heav'n's decree, fhe goes
To find her death among forbidden foes ;   880
Haft with thefe arms, and take thy fteepy flight,
Where, with the gods adverfe, the Latins fight :
This bow to thee, this quiver I bequeath,
This chofen arrow to revenge her death :
By whate'er hand Camilla fhall be flain,   885
Or of the Trojan, or Italian train,
Let him not pafs unpunifh'd from the plain.
Then in a hollow cloud, myfelf will aid,
To bear the breathlefs body of my maid :
Unfpoil'd fhall be her arms, and unprophan'd 890
Her holy limbs with any human hand :
And in a marble tomb laid in her native land.

   She faid : the faithful nymph defcends from
                      [high
With rapid flight, and cuts the founding fky :
Black clouds and ftormy winds around her body
                      [fly.j

By this, the Trojan and the Tufcan horfe,   896
Drawn up in fquadrons, with united force,

Approach the walls ; the fprightly courfers bound ;
Prefs forward on their bitts, and fhift their ground :
Shields, arms, and fpears, flafh horribly from far ;
And the fields glitter with a waving war.   901
Oppos'd to thefe, come on with furious force
Meffapus, Coras, and the Latian horfe ;
Thefe in the body plac'd ; on either hand
Suftain'd, and clos'd by fair Camilla's band.   905
Advancing in a line, they couch their fpears ;
And lefs and lefs the middle fpace appears.
Thick fmoke obfcures the field : and fcarce are feen
The neighing courfers, and the fhouting men.
In diftance of their darts they ftop their courfe ;   910
Then man to man they rufh, and horfe to horfe.
The face of heav'n their flying jav'lins hide :
And deaths unfeen are dealt on either fide.
Tyrrhenus, and Aconteus, void of fear,
By mettled courfers borne in full career,   915
Meet firft oppos'd : and, with a mighty fhock,
Their horfes heads againft each other knock.
Far from his fteed is fierce Aconteus caft ;
As with an engine's force, or lightning's blaft :
He rolls along in blood, and breathes his laft.   920

The Latin fquadrons take a fudden fright;
And fling their fhields behind, to fave their backs in
[flight.

Spurring at fpeed to their own walls they drew;
Clofe in the rear the Tufcan troops purfue:
And urge their flight, Afylas leads the chafe; 925
Till feiz'd with fhame they wheel about, and face:
Receive their foes, and raife a threat'ning cry.
The Tufcans take their turn to fear and fly.

So fwelling furges, with a thund'ring roar,
Driv'n on each other's backs, infult the fhore; 930
Bound o'er the rocks, incroach upon the land;
And far upon the beach eject the fand.
Then backward with a fwing, they take their way;
Repuls'd from upper ground, and feek their mother-
[fea:

With equal hurry quit th' invaded fhore; 935
And fwallow back the fand, and ftones they fpew'd
e   fore.

Twice were the Tufcans mafter of the field,
Twice by the Latins, in their turn, repell'd.
Afham'd at length, to the third charge they ran,
Both hofts refolv'd, and mingled man to man: 940
Now dying groans are heard, the fields are ftrow'd
With falling bodies, and are drunk with blood:

Arms, horfes, men, on heaps together lie :
Confus'd the fight, and more confus'd the cry.
Orfilochus, who durft not prefs too near   945
Strong Remulus, at diftance drove his fpear ;
And ftruck the fteel beneath his horfe's ear.
The fiery fteed, impatient of the wound,
Curvets, and fpringing upward with a bound,
His hopelefs lord caft backward on the ground. 950
Catillus pierc'd Iolas firft; then drew
His reeking lance, and at Herminius threw :
The mighty champion of the Tufcan crew.
His neck and throat unarm'd, his head was bare,
But fhaded with a length of yellow hair :   955
Secure, he fought, expos'd on ev'ry part,
A fpacious mark for fwords, and for the flying dart :
Acrofs the fhoulders came the feather'd wound ;
Transfix'd, he fell, and doubled to the ground.
  The fands with ftreaming blood are fanguine dy'd ;
And death with honour, fought on either fide. 961
  Refiftlefs thro' the war, Camilla rode ;
In danger unappall'd, and pleas'd with blood.
One fide was bare for her exerted breaft ;
One fhoulder with her painted quiver prefs'd. 965

H 4

Now from afar her fatal jav'lins play;
Now with her axe's edge she hews her way;
Diana's arms upon her shoulder found;
And when, too closely press'd, she quits the ground;
From her bent bow she sends a backward wound.
Her maids, in martial pomp, on either side, 971
Larina, Tulla, fierce Tarpeia ride;
Italians all: in peace, their queen's delight:
In war, the bold companions of the fight.

　So march'd the Thracian Amazons of old, 975
When Thermodon with bloody billows roll'd;
Such troops as these in shining arms were seen,
When Theseus met in fight their maiden queen:
Such to the field Penthesilea led,
From the fierce virgin when the Grecians fled: 980
With such, return'd triumphant from the war;
Her maids with cries attend the lofty carr:
They clash with manly force their moony shields:
With female shouts resound the Phrygian fields.

　Who foremost, and who last, heroick maid, 985
On the cold earth were by thy courage laid?
Thy spear, of mountain-ash, Eumenius first,
With fury driv'n, from side to side transpierc'd;
A purple stream came spouting from the wound;
Bath'd in his blood he lies, and bites the ground. 990

Lyris and Pegafus at once fhe flew ;
The former, as the flacken'd reins he drew,
Of his faint fteed : the latter, as he ftretch'd
His arm to prop his friend, the jav'lin reach'd.
By the fame weapon, fent from the fame hand, 995
Both fall together, and both fpurn the fand.
Amaftrus next is added to the flain :
The reft in rout fhe follows o'er the plain :
Tereus, Harpalicus, Demophoon,
And Chromys, at full fpeed her fury fhun.   1000
Of all her deadly darts, not one fhe loft ;
Each was attended with a Trojan ghoft.
Young Ornithus beftrode a hunter fteed,
Swift for the chafe, and of Apulian breed ;
Him, from afar, fhe fpy'd in arms unknown ; 1005
O'er his broad back an ox's hide was thrown :
His helm a wolf, whofe gaping jaws were fpread
A cov'ring for hischeeks, and grinn'd around his head.
He clench'd within his hand an iron prong ;
And tower'd above the reft, confpicuous in the throng.
Him foon fhe fingled from the flying train,   1011
And flew with eafe : then thus infults the flain.
Vain hunter, didft thou think thro' woods to chafe
The favage herd, a vile and trembling race ?

H 5

Here ceafe thy vaunts, and own my victory ; 1015
A woman-warrior was too ftrong for thee.
Yet if the ghofts demand the conqu'ror's name,
Confeffing great Camilla, fave thy fhame.
Then Butes, and Orfilochus fhe flew,
The bulkieft bodies of the Trojan crew.   1020
But Butes breaft to breaft : the fpear defcends
Above the gorget, where his helmet ends,
And o'er the fhield which his left fide defends.
Orfilochus, and fhe, their courfers ply,
He feems to follow, and fhe feems to fly.   1025
But in a narrower ring fhe makes the race;
And then he flies, and fhe purfues the chafe.
Gath'ring at length on her deluded foe,
She fwings her ax, and rifes at the blow:
Full on the helm behind, with fuch a fway   1030
The weapon falls, the riven fteel gives way :
He groans, he roars, he fues in vain for grace;
Brains, mingled with his blood, befmear his face.
Aftonif'd Aunus juft arrives by chance,
To fee his fall, nor farther dares advance :
But fixing on the horrid maid his eye,
He ftares, and fhakes, and finds it vain to fly.
Yet like a true Ligurian, born to cheat,
(At leaft while fortune favour'd his deceit)

Cries out aloud, what courage have you fhown, 1040
Who truft your courfer's ftrength, and not your own?
Forego the 'vantage of your horfe, alight,
And then on equal terms begin the fight:
It fhall be feen, weak woman, what you can,
When, foot to foot, you combat with a man. 1045
He faid: fhe glows with anger and difdain,
Difmounts with fpeed to dare him on the plain :
And leaves her horfe at large among her train.
With her drawn fword defies him to the field ;
And marching, lifts aloft her maiden fhield : 1050
The youth, who thought his cunning did fucceed,
Reins round his horfe, and urges all his fpeed,
Adds the remembrance of the fpur, and hides
The goring rowels in his bleeding fides.
Vain fool, and coward, faid the lofty maid, 1055
Caught in the train, which thou thyfelf haft laid.!
On others practife thy Ligurian arts ;
Thin ftratagems, and tricks of little hearts
Are loft on me. Nor fhalt thou fafe retire,
With vaunting lies to thy fallacious fire. 1060
At this, fo faft her flying feet fhe fped,
That foon fhe ftrain'd beyond his horfe's head:

H 6

Then turning fhort, at once fhe feiz'd the rein,
And laid the boafter grov'ling on the plain.

Not with more eafe the falcon from above,   1065
Truffes, in middle air, the trembling dove:
Then plumes the prey, in her ftrong pounces bound ;
The feathers foul with blood come tumbling to the
                                                [ground.

Now mighty Jove, from his fuperior height,
With his broad eye furveys th' unequal fight. 1070
He fires the breaft of Ta'chon with difdain ;
And fends him to redeem th' abandon'd plain.
Between the broken ranks the Tufcan rides,
And thefe encourages, and thofe he chides :
Recalls each leader, by his name, from flight; 1075
Renews their ardor, and reftores the fight.
What panick fear has feiz'd your fouls ? O fhame,
O brand perpetual of th' Etrurian name ;
Cowards, incurable ! a woman's hand
Drives, breaks, and fcatters your ignoble band ! 1080
Now caft away the fword, and quit the fhield :
What ufe of weapons which you dare not wield ?
Not thus you fly your female foes, by night,
Nor fhun the feaft, when the full bowls invite :
When to fat off'rings the glad augur calls ;   1085
And the fhrill horn-pipe founds to bacchanals.

Thefe are your ftudy'd cares ; your lewd delight :
Swift to debauch ; but flow to manly fight.
Thus having faid, he fpurs amid the foes ;
Not managing the life he meant to lofe.   1090
The firft he found he feiz'd, with headlong hafte,
In his ftrong gripe : and clafp'd around the wafte :
'Twas Venulus ; whom from his horfe he tore,
And (laid athwart his own) in triumph bore.
Loud fhouts enfue : the Latins turn their eyes, 1095
And view th' unufual fight with vaft furprize.
The fiery Tarchon, flying o'er the plains,
Prefs'd in his arms the pond'rous prey fuftains :
Then with his fhorten'd fpear, explores around
His jointed arms, to fix a deadly wound.   1100
Nor lefs the captive ftruggles for his life :
He writhes his body to prolong the ftrife :
And, fencing for his naked throat, exerts
His utmoft vigour, and the point averts.

So ftoops the yellow eagle from on high,   1105
And bears a fpeckled ferpent thro' the fky ;
Faft'ning his crooked talons on the prey ;
The pris'ner hiffes thro' the liquid way :
Refifts the royal hawk, and tho' oppreft,
She fights in volumes, and erects her creft.   1110

Turn'd to her foe, fhe ftiffens ev'ry fcale;
And fhoots her forky tongue, and whifks her threat—
['ning tail.
Againft the victor all defence is weak;
Th' imperial bird ftill plies her with his beak:
He tears her bowels, and her breaft he gores;   1115
Then claps his pinions, and fecurely foars.

Thus, thro' the midft of circling enemies,
Strong Tarchon fnatch'd, and bore away his prize:
The Tyrrhene troops, that fhrunk before, now prefs
The Latins, and prefume the like fuccefs.   1120

Then Aruns, doom'd to death, his arts effay'd
To murder, unefpy'd, the Volfcian maid:
This way and that his winding courfe he bends:
And wherefoe'er fhe turns, her fteps attends.
When fhe retires victorious from the chafe,   1125
He wheels about with care, and fhifts his place:
When rufhing on, fhe feeks her foes in fight.
He keeps aloof, but keeps her ftill in fight:
He threats, and trembles, trying ev'ry way:
Unfeen to kill, and fafely to betray.   1130

Chloreus, the prieft of Cybele, from far,
Glitt'ring in Phrygian arms amidft the war,
Was by the virgin view'd: the fteed he prefs'd
Was proud with trappings, and his brawny cheft

With fcales of gilded brafs was cover'd o'er :   1135
A robe of Tyrian dye the rider wore.
With deadly wounds he gaul'd the diftant foe;
Gnoffian his fhafts, and Lycian was his bow :
A golden helm his front, and head furrounds;
A gilded quiver from his fhoulder founds.   1140
Gold, weav'd with linen, on his thighs he wore; ⎫
With flowers of needlework diftinguifh'd o'er :   ⎬
With golden buckles bound, and gather'd up before.⎭
Him, the fierce maid beheld, with ardent eyes;
Fond and ambitious of fo rich a prize :   1145
Or that the temple might his trophies hold,
Or elfe to fhine herfelf in Trojan gold :
Blind in her hafte, fhe chafes him alone,
And feeks his life, regardlefs of her own.
This lucky moment the fly traitor chofe :   1150 ⎫
Then, ftarting from his ambufh, up he rofe,   ⎬
And threw, but firft to heav'n addrefs'd his vows. ⎭
O patron of Soractes' high abodes,
Phœbus, the ruling pow'r among the gods;
Whom firft we ferve, whole woods of unctuous pine
Are fell'd for thee, and to thy glory fhine;   1156
By thee protected, with our naked fouls,
Thro' flames unfing'd we march, and tread the kindled,
                                    [coals:

Give me, propitious pow'r, to wash away

The stains of this dishonourable day :   1160

Nor spoils, nor triumph, from the fact I claim;

But with my future actions trust my fame.

Let me, by stealth, this female plague o'ercome;

And from the field return inglorious home.

Apollo heard, and granting half his pray'r, 1165

Shuffled in winds the rest, and tofs'd in empty air.

He gives the death defir'd; his safe return,

By southern tempests to the seas is born.

Now, when the jav'lin whiz'd along the skies,

Both armies on Camilla turn'd their eyes,   1170

Directed by the sound : of either host,

Th' unhappy virgin, tho' concern'd the most,

Was only deaf; so greedy was she bent

On golden spoils, and on her prey intent :

Till in her pap the winged weapon stood   1175

Infix'd; and deeply drunk the purple blood.

Her sad attendants hasten to sustain

Their dying lady drooping on the plain.

Far from their sight the trembling Aruns flies,

With beating heart, and fear confus'd with joys :

Nor dares he farther to pursue his blow;   1181

Or ev'n to bear the sight of his expiring foe.

As when the wolf has torn a bullock's hide,
At unawares, or ranch'd a shepherd's side :
Confcious of his audacious deed, he flies, 1185
And claps his quiv'ring tail between his thighs ;
So, fpeeding once, the wretch no more attends ;
But fpurring forward herds among his friends.
She wrench'd the jav'lin with her dying hands ;
But wedg'd within her breaft the weapon ftands : 1190
The wood fhe draws, the fteely point remains ;
She ftaggers in her feat with agonizing pains :
A gath'ring mift o'erclouds her chearful eyes ;
And from her cheeks the rofy colour flies.
Then turns to her, whom, of her female train 1195
She trufted moft, and thus fhe fpeaks with pain.
Acca, 'tis paft ! he fwims before my fight,
Inexorable death ; and claims his right.
Bear my laft words to Turnus, fly with fpeed,
And bid him timely to my charge fucceed : 1200
Repel the Trojans, and the town relieve :
Farewel ; and in this kifs my parting breath receive
She faid ; and fliding funk upon the plain ;
Dying, her open'd hand forfakes the rein ; 1204
Short, and more fhort, fhe pants : by flow degrees
Her mind the paffage from her body frees.

She drops her fword, fhe neds her plumy creft;
Her drooping head declining on her breaft:
In the laft figh her ftruggling foul expires;   1209
And murm'ringwith difdain,toStygianfoundsretires.

A fhout, that ftruck the golden ftars, enfu'd:
Defpair and rage, and languifh'd fight renew'd.
The Trojan troops, and Tufcans in a line,
Advance to charge; the mix'd Arcadians join.

But Cynthia's maid, high feated, from afar 1215
Surveys the field, and fortune of the war:
Unmov'd a while, till proftrate on the plain,
Welt'ring in blood, fhe fees Camilla flain;
And round her corps, of friends and foes a fight-
                                        ing train.

Then, from the bottom of her breaft, fhe drew 1220
A mournful figh, and thefe fad words enfue:
Too dear a fine, ah much lamented maid,
For warring with the Trojans, thou haft paid!
Nor ought avail'd, in this unhappy ftrife,
Diana's facred arms, to fave thy life.   1225
Yet unreveng'd thy goddefs will not leave
Her vot'ry's death, nor with vain forrow grieve.
Branded the wretch, and be his name abhorr'd;
But after ages fhall thy praife record.

Th' inglorious coward foon fhall prefs the plain; 1230
Thus vows thy queen, and thus the fates ordain.

High o'er the field, there ftood a hilly mound;
Sacred the place, and fpread with oaks around;
Where in a marble tomb, Dercennus lay,   1235
A king that once in Latium bore the fway.
The beauteous Opis thither bent her flight,
To mark the traitor Aruns from the height.
Him, in refulgent arms, fhe foon efpy'd,
Swoln with fuccefs, and loudly thus fhe cry'd.
Thy backward fteps, vain boafter, are too late; 1240
Turn, like a man at length, and meet thy fate.
Charg'd with my meffage to Camilla go;
And fay I fent thee to the fhades below;
An honour undeferv'd from Cynthia's bow.

She faid: and from her quiver chofe with fpeed
The winged fhaft, predeftin'd for the deed: 1246
Then to the ftubborn eugh her ftrength apply'd:
Till the far diftant horns approach'd on either fide.
The bow-ftring touch'd her breaft, fo ftrong fhe drew;
Whizzing in air the fatal arrow flew.   1250
At once the twanging bow, and founding dart,
The traitor heard, and felt the point within his heart.
Him, beating with his heels, in pangs of death,
His flying friends to foreign fields bequeath.

The conqu'ring damfel, with expanded wings, 1255
The welcome meffage to her miftrefs brings.

   Their leader loft, the Volfcians quit the field ;
And, unfuftain'd, the chiefs of Turnus yield.
The frighted foldiers, when their captains fly,
More on their fpeed than on their ftrength rely. 1260
Confus'd in flight, they bear each other down ;
And fpur their horfes headlong to the town.
Driv'n by their foes, and to their fears refign'd,
Not once they turn ; but take their wounds behind.
Thefe drop the fhield, and thofe the lance forego; 1265
Or on their fhoulders bear the flacken'd bow.
The hoofs of horfes with a rattling found,
Beat fhort, and thick, and fhake the rotten ground.
Black clouds of duft come rolling in the fky,
And o'er the darken'd walls, and rampires fly. 1270
The trembling matrons, from their lofty ftands,
Rend heav'n with female fhrieks, and wring their hands.
All preffing on, purfuers and purfu'd,
Are crufh'd in crowds, a mingled multitude.
Some happy few efcape: the throng too late 1275
Rufh on for entrance, till they choke the gate.
Ev'n in the fight of home, the wretched fire
Looks on, and fees his helplefs fon expire.

Then, in a fright, the folding gates they clofe:
But leave their friends excluded with their foes. 1288
The vanquifh'd cry; the victors loudly fhout;
'Tis terror all within; and flaughter all without.
Blind in their fear, they bounce againft the wall,
Or to the moats purfu'd, precipitate their fall.

   The Latian virgins, valiant with defpair, 1285
Arm'd on the tow'rs the common danger fhare:
So much of zeal their country's caufe infpir'd;
So much Camilla's great example fir'd.
Poles, fharpen'd in the flames, from high they throw;
With imitated darts to gaul the foe.   8290
Their lives, for godlike freedom they bequeath;
And crowd each other to be firft in death.
Mean time to Turnus, ambufh'd in the fhade,
With heavy tidings, came th' unhappy maid.
The Volfcians overthrown, Camilla kill'd,   1295
The foes intirely mafters of the field,
Like a refiftlefs flood, come rolling on:
The cry goes off the plain, and thickens to the town.
   Inflam'd with rage, (for fo the furies fire
The Daunian's breaft, and fo the fates require,) 1300
He leaves the hilly pafs, the woods in vain
Poffefs'd, and downward iffues on the plain:

Scarce was he gone, when to the ftraights, now freed
From fecret foes, the Trojan troops fucceed.
Thro' the black foreft, and the ferny brake,   1305
Unknowingly fecure, their way they take.
From the rough mountains to the plain defcend;
And there, in order drawn, their line extend.
Both armies, now, in open fields are feen :
Nor far the diftance of the fpace between.   1310
Both to the city bend: Æneas fees,
Thro' fmoaking fields, his haft'ning enemies.
And Turnus views the Trojans in array,
And hears th' approaching horfes proudly neigh.
Soon had their hofts in bloody battle join'd ;   1315
But weftward to the fea the fun declin'd.
Intrench'd before the town, both armies lie :
While night with fable wings involves the fky.

THE

TWELFTH BOOK

OF THE

ÆNEIS.

THE

ARGUMENT.

*TURNUS challenges Æneas to a single combat:
articles are agreed on, but broken by the Rutuli,
who wound Æneas: he is miraculously cur'd by Venus,
forces Turnus to a duel, and concludes the poem with
his death.*

The Twelfth Book of the

Æ N E I S.

WHEN Turnus saw the Latins leave the field;
Their armies broken, and their courage
[quell'd;
Himself become the mark of publick spight,
His honour question'd for the promis'd fight:
The more he was with vulgar hate opprefs'd,   5
The more his fury boil'd within his breaft:
He rous'd his vigour for the late debate;
And rais'd his haughty soul, to meet his fate.
As when the swains the Libyan lion chafe,
He makes a four retreat, nor mends his pace: 10
But if the pointed jav'lin pierce his side,
The lordly beaft returns with double pride;
He wrenches out the steel, he roars for pain;
His sides he lashes, and erects his mane:

So Turnus fares, his eye-balls flash with fire,   15
Thro' his wide nostrils clouds of smoak expire.

Trembling with rage, around the court he ran;
At length approach'd the king, and thus began.
No more excuses or delays: I stand
In arms prepar'd to combat, hand to hand,   20
This base deserter of his native land.
The Trojan, by his word, is bound to take
The same conditions which himself did make.
Renew the truce, the solemn rites prepare;
And to my single virtue trust the war.   25
The Latians unconcern'd shall see the fight;
This arm unaided shall assert your right:
Then, if my prostrate body press the plain,
To him the crown, and beauteous bride remain.

To whom the king sedately thus reply'd;   30
Brave youth, the more your valour has been try'd,
The more becomes it us, with due respect
To weigh the chance of war, which you neglect.
You want not wealth, or a successive throne,
Or cities, which your arms have made your own;   35
My towns and treasures are at your command;
And stor'd with blooming beauties is my land:
Laurentum more than one Lavinia sees,
Unmarry'd, fair, of noble families.

Now let me fpeak, and you with patience hear, 40
Things which perhaps may grate a lover's ear :
But found advice, proceeding from a heart
Sincerely yours, and free from fraudful art.

The gods, by figns, have manifeftly fhown,
No prince, Italian born, fhould heir my throne : 45
Oft have our augurs, in prediction fkill'd,
And oft our priefts, a foreign fon reveal'd.
Yet, won by worth, that cannot be withftood,
Brib'd by my kindnefs to my kindred blood,
Urg'd by my wife, who wou'd not be deny'd, 50
I promis'd my Lavinia for your bride :
Her from her plighted lord by force I took ;
All ties of treaties, and of honour broke :
On your account I wag'd an impious war,
With what fuccefs 'tis needlefs to declare ; 55
I and my fubjects feel ; and you have had your fhare.
Twice vanquifh'd, while in bloody fields we ftrive,
Scarce in our walls, we keep our hopes alive ;
The rolling flood runs warm with human gore ;
The bones of Latians glance the neighb'ring fhore: 60
Why put I not an end to this debate,
Still unrefolv'd, and ftill a flave to fate ?

If Turnus' death a lasting peace can give,
Why should not I procure it whilst you live?
Shou'd I to doubtful arms your youth betray,   65
What wou'd my kinsmen, the Rutulians, say?
And should you fall in fight, (which heav'n defend) ⎫
How curse the cause, which hasten'd to his end   ⎬
The daughter's lover, and the father's friend?   ⎭
Weigh in your mind, the various chance of war, 70
Pity your parent's age; and ease his care.

　Such balmy words he pour'd, but all in vain;
The proffer'd med'cine but provok'd the pain.
The wrathful youth disdaining the relief,
With intermitting sobs, thus vents his grief: 75
Thy care, O best of fathers, which you take
For my concerns, at my desire forsake.
Permit me not to languish out my days;
But make the best exchange of life for praise.
This arm, this lance, can well dispute the prize; 80
And the blood follows, where the weapon flies;
His goddess mother is not near, to shrowd
The flying coward with an empty cloud.

　But now the queen, who fear'd for Turnus' life,
And loath'd the hard conditions of the strife, 85
Held him by force; and, dying in his death,
In these sad accents gave her sorrow breath.

O Turnus, I adjure thee by thefe tears;
And whate'er price Amata's honour bears
Within thy breaft, fince thou art all my hope,   90
My fickly mind's repofe, my finking age's prop;
Since on the fafety of thy life alone
Depends Latinus, and the Latian throne:
Refufe me not this one, this only pray'r;
To wave the combat, and purfue the war.   95
Whatever chance attends this fatal ftrife,
Think it includes in thine Amata's life.
I cannot live a flave; or fee my throne
Ufurp'd by ftrangers, or a Trojan fon.

At this, a flood of tears Lavinia fhed;   100
A crimfon blufh her beauteous face o'erfpread,
Varying her cheeks by turns, with white and red.
The driving colours, never at a ftay,
Run here and there; and flufh, and fade away.
Delightful change! thus Indian iv'ry fhows,   105
Which with the bord'ring paint of purple glows;
Or lilies damafk'd by the neighb'ring rofe.
The lover gaz'd, and burning with defire:
The more he look'd, the more he fed the fire:
Revenge, and jealous rage, and fecret fpight,   110
Roll in his breaft, and rouze him to the fight.

I 3

Then fixing on the queen his ardent eyes,
Firm to his firſt intent, he thus replies.
O mother, do not by your tears prepare
Such boding omens, and prejudge the war.   115
Reſolv'd on fight, I am no longer free
To ſhun my death, if heav'n my death decree.

Then turning to the herald, thus purſues;
Go, greet the Trojans with ungrateful news.
Denounce from me, that when to-morrow's light 120
Shall gild the heav'ns, he need not urge the fight:
The Trojan and Rutulian troops no more
Shall dye, with mutual blood, the Latian ſhore:
Our ſingle ſwords the quarrel ſhall decide,
And to the victor be the beauteous bride.   125

He ſaid, and ſtriding on, with ſpeedy pace
He ſought his courſers of the Thracian race.
At his approach, they toſs their heads on high;
And proudly neighing, promiſe victory.
The ſires of theſe Orithia ſent from far   130
To grace Pilumnus, when he went to war.
The drifts of Thracian ſnows were ſcarce ſo white,
Nor northern winds in fleetneſs match'd their flight.

Officious grooms ftand ready by his fide;   134
And fome with combs their flowing manes divide,
And others ftroke their chefts, and gently footh
                                    [their pride.

He fheath'd his limbs in arms; a temper'd mafs
Of golden metal thofe, and mountain brafs.
Then to his head his glitt'ring helm he ty'd;
And girt his faithful fauchion to his fide.   140
In his Æmean forge the god of fire
That fauchion labour'd for the hero's fire:
Immortal keennefs on the blade beftow'd,
And plung'd it hiffing in the Stygian flood.
Prop'd on a pillar, which the cieling bore,   145
Was plac'd the lance Auruncan Actor wore;
Which with fuch force he brandifh'd in his hand,
The tough afh trembled like an ofier wand.
Then cry'd, O pond'rous fpoil of Actor flain,
And never yet by Turnus tofs'd in vain,   150
Fail not this day thy wonted force: but go,
Sent by this hand, to pierce the Trojan foe:
Give me to tear his corflet from his breaft,
And from that eunuch head, to rend the creft:
Drag'd in the duft, his frizled hair to foil,   155
Hot from the vexing ir'n, and fmear'd with fragrant oil.

Thus while he raves, from his wide noſtrils flies
A fiery ſteam, and ſparkles from his eyes.
So fares the bull in his lov'd female's ſight;
Proudly he bellows, and preludes the fight :   160
He tries his goring horns againſt a tree :
And meditates his abſent enemy :
He puſhes at the winds, he digs the ſtrand
With his black hoofs, and ſpurns the yellow ſand.
    Nor leſs the Trojan, in his Lemnian arms, 165
To future fight his manly courage warms :
He whets his fury, and with joy prepares,
To terminate at once the ling'ring wars.
To chear his chiefs, and tender ſon, relates
What heav'n had promis'd, and expounds the
                                              [fates. 170
Then to the Latian king he ſends, to ceaſe
The rage of arms, and ratify the peace.
    The morn' enſuing from the mountains height,
Had ſcarcely ſpread the ſkies with roſy light;
Th' ethereal courſers bounding from the ſea,   175
From out their flaming noſtrils breath'd the day :
When now the Trojan and Rutulian guard,
In friendly labour join'd, the liſt prepar'd.

Beneath the walls, they measure out the space; 179 ⎤
Then sacred altars rear, on sods of grass; |
Where, with religious rites, their common gods they ⎬
                                          [place. ⎦

In purest white, the priests their heads attire,
And living waters bear and holy fire:
And o'er their linen hoods, and shaded hair,
Long twisted wreaths of sacred vervain wear.   185

  In order issuing from the town appears
The Latin legion, arm'd with pointed spears;
And from the fields, advancing on a line,
The Trojan and the Tuscan forces join:
Their various arms afford a pleasing sight: 190
A peaceful train they seem, in peace prepar'd for fight.
  Betwixt the ranks the proud commanders ride,
Glitt'ring with gold, and vests in purple dy'd.
Here Mneftheus, author of the Memmian line,
And there Messapus born of seed divine.   195
The sign is giv'n, and round the lifted space,
Each man in order fills his proper place.
Reclining on their ample shields, they stand;
And fix their pointed lances in the sand.
Now, studious of the fight, a num'rous throng 200
Of either sex promiscuous, old and young,

I 5

Swarm from the town : by thofe who reft behind;.
The gates and walls, and houfes tops are lin'd.

Mean time the queen of heav'n beheld the fight,
With eyes unpleas'd,   from   mount   Albano's
                                    [height : 205
(Since call'd Albano, by fucceeding fame,
But then an empty hill, without a name.)
She thence furvey'd the field, the Trojan pow'rs,
The Latian fquadrons, and Laurentine tow'rs.
Then thus the goddefs of the fkies befpake,   210
With fighs and tears, the goddefs of the lake ;
King Turnus' fifter, once a lovely maid,
Ere to the luft of lawlefs Jove betray'd,
Comprefs'd by force, but by the grateful god;
Now made the Naïs of the neighb'ring flood. 215

O nymph, the pride of living lakes, faid fhe,
O moft renown'd, and moft belov'd by me,
Long haft thou known, nor need I to record
The wanton fallies of my wand'ring lord :
Of ev'ry Latian fair, whom Jove mifled,   220
To mount by ftealth my violated bed;
To thee alone I grudg'd not his embrace ;
But give a part of heav'n, and an unenvy'd place.
Now learn from me, thy near approaching grief,
Nor think my wifhes want to thy relief.   225

While fortune favour'd, nor heav'n's king deny'd,
To lend my fuccour to the Latian fide,
I fav'd thy brother, and the finking ftate;
But now he ftruggles with unequal fate;
And goes with gods averfe, o'ermatch'd in ⎞
              [might, 230 ⎟
To meet inevitable death in fight: ⎬
Nor muft I break the truce, nor can fuftain the ⎟
              fight. ⎠

Thou, if thou dar'ft, thy prefent aid fupply;
It well becomes a fifter's care to try.

    At this the lovely nymph, with grief oppref's'd, 135
Thrice tore her hair, and beat her comely breaft.
To whom Saturnia thus; thy tears are late:
Hafte, fnatch him, if he can be fnatch'd, from fate.
New tumults kindle, violate the truce;
Who knows what changeful fortune may pro-
              [duce? 240
'Tis not a crime t' attempt what I decree,
Or if it were, difcharge the crime on me.
She faid, and, failing on the winged wind,
Left the fad nymph fufpended in her mind.

    And now in pomp the peaceful kings appear: 245
Four fteeds the chariot of Latinus bear:

             I 6

Twelve golden beams around his temples play,
To mark his lineage from the god of day.
Two fnowy courfers Turnus' chariot yoke,
And in his hand two maffy fpears he fhook: 250
Then iffu'd from the camp, in arms divine,
Æneas, author of the Roman line:
And by his fide Afcanius took his place,
The fecond hope of Rome's immortal race.   :
Adorn'd in white, a rev'rend prieft appears ; 255 ⎫
And off'rings to the flaming altars bears ;   ⎬
A porket, and a lamb, that never fuffer'd fhears.⎭
Then, to the rifing fun he turns his eyes,
And fhews the beafts defign'd for facrifice,
With falt, and meal: with like officious care   260
He marks their foreheads, and he clips their hair.
Betwixt their horns the purple wine he fheds,
With the fame gen'rous juice the flame he feeds.
Æneas then unfheath'd his fhining fword,
And thus with pious pray'rs the gods ador'd.   265
    All-feeing fun, and thou Aufonian foil,
For which I have fuftain'd fo long a toil,
Thou king of heav'n, and thou the queen of air,
(Propitious now, and reconcil'd by pray'r,)
Thou god of war, whofe unrefifted fway   270
The labours and events of arms obey ;

Ye living fountains, and ye running floods,
All pow'rs of ocean, all ethereal gods,
Hear, and bear record : if I fall in field,
Or recreant in the fight, to Turnus yield,   ·275
My Trojans fhall increafe Evander's town ;
Afcanious fhall renounce the Aufonian crown ;
All claims, all queftions of debate fhall ceafe ;
Nor he, nor they, with force infringe the peace.
But if my jufter arms prevail in fight,   · 280
As fure they fhall, if I divine aright,
My Trojans fhall not o'er th' Italians reign :
Both equal, both unconquer'd fhall remain :
Join'd in their laws, their lands, and their abodes ;
I afk but altars for my weary gods.   285
The care of thofe religious rites be mine :
The crown to king Latinus I refign ;
His be the fov'reign fway.   Nor will I fhare
His pow'r in peace, or his command in war.
For me, my friends another town fhall frame, 290
And blefs the rifing tow'rs, with fair Lavinia's name.
    Thus he.   Then with erected eyes and hands,
The Latian king before his altar ftands.
By the fame heav'n, faid he, and earth, and main,
And all the pow'rs, that all the three contain ; 295

By hell below, and by that upper god,

Whose thunder signs the peace, who seals it with his
[nod;

So let Latona's double offspring hear,

And double-fronted Janus what I swear :

I touch the sacred altars, touch the flames,   300

And all those pow'rs attest, and all their names :

Whatever chance befall on either side,

No term of time this union shall divide :

No force, no fortune, shall my vows unbind,

Or shake the stedfast tenour of my mind :   305.

Not tho' the circling seas shou'd break their bound,

O'erflow the shores, or sap the solid ground;

Not tho' the lamps of heav'n their spheres forsake,

Hurl'd down, and hissing in the nether lake :

Ev'n as this royal scepter, (for he bore   310

A scepter in his hand) shall never more

Shoot out in branches, or renew the birth ;

(An orphan now, cut from the mother earth.

By the keen ax, dishonour'd of its hair,

And cas'd in brass, for Latian kings to bear.) 315

When thus in publick view the peace was ty'd.

With solemn vows, and sworn on either side,

All dues perform'd which holy rites require ;

The victim beasts are slain before the fire :

The trembling entrails from their bodies torn, 320
And to the fatten'd flames in chargers borne.

　Already the Rutulians deem their man
O'ermatch'd in arms, before the fight began.
Firſt riſing fears are whiſper'd thro' the crowd;
Then, gath'ring ſound, they murmur more aloud. 325
Now ſide to ſide, they meaſure with their eyes
The champions bulk, their ſinews and their ſize :
The nearer they approach, the more is known.
Th' apparent diſadvantage of their own.
Turnus himſelf appears in publick ſight　　330
Conſcious of fate, deſponding of the fight.
Slowly he moves; and at his altar ſtands
With eyes dejeƈted, and with trembling hands :
And while he mutters undiſtinguiſh'd pray'rs,
A livid deadneſs in his cheeks appears.　　335

　With anxious pleaſure when Juturna view'd
Th' increaſing fright of the mad multitude,
When their ſhort ſighs, and thickning ſobs ſhe heard,
And found their ready minds for change prepar'd;
Diſſembling her immortal form, ſhe took　　340
Camertus' mien, his habit, and his look,
A chief of ancient blood : in arms well known
Was his great ſire, and he, his greater ſon.

His shape assum'd, amid the ranks she ran,
And humouring their first motions, thus began. 345

For shame, Rutulians, can you bear the sight
Of one expos'd for all, in single fight?
Can we, before the face of heav'n confess
Our courage colder, or our numbers less?
View all the Trojan host, th' Arcadian band, 350
And Tuscan army; count 'em as they stand:
Undaunted to the battle if we go,
Scarce ev'ry second man will share a foe.
Turnus, 'tis true, in this unequal strife
Shall lose, with honour, his devoted life: 355
Or change it rather for immortal fame,
Succeeding to the gods, from whence he came:
But you, a servile, and inglorious band,
For foreign lords shall sow your native land:
Those fruitful fields, your fighting fathers gain'd, 360
Which have so long their lazy sons sustain'd.

With words like these, she carry'd her design;
A rising murmur runs along the line.
Then ev'n the city troops, and Latians, tir'd
With tedious war, seem with new souls inspir'd: 265
Their champion's fate with pity they lament;
And of the league, so lately sworn, repent.

Nor fails the goddess to foment the rage
With lying wonders, and a false presage:
But adds a sign, which, present to their eyes, 370
Inspires new courage, and a glad surprize.
For, sudden, in the fiery tracts above,
Appears in pomp th' imperial bird of Jove:
A plump of fowl he spies, that swim the lakes;
And o'er their heads his sounding pinions shakes. 375
Then stooping on the faireft of the train,
In his strong tallons truss'd a silver swan.
Th' Italians wonder at th' unusual sight;
But while he lags, and labours in his flight,
Behold the daftard fowl return anew;   380
And with united force the foe pursue:
Clam'rous around the royal hawk they fly;
And thick'ning in a cloud, o'erfhade the sky.
They cuff, they scratch, they cross his airy course;
Nor can th' incumber'd bird sustain their force: 385
But vex'd, not vanquifh'd, drops the pond'rous prey:
And, lighten'd of his burden, wings his way.

  Th' Aufonian bands with shouts salute the fight:
Eager of action, and demand the fight.
Then king Tolumnius, vers'd in augurs' arts, 390
Cries out, and thus his boafted skill imparts.

At length 'tis granted,. what I long defir'd;·

This, this is what my frequent vows requir'd.

Ye gods, I take your omen, and obey:

Advance, my friends, and charge, I lead the way. 395

Thefe are the foreign foes, whofe impious band,

Like that rapacious bird, infeft our land :

But foon, like him, they fhall be forc'd to fea

By ftrength united, and forego the prey;

Your timely fuccour to your country bring;   400

Hafte to the refcue; and redeem your king.

He faid : and preffing onward, thro' the crew,.

Pois'd in his lifted arm, his lance he threw:

The winged weapon, whiftling in the wind,·

Came driving on, nor mifs'd the mark defign'd. 405

At once the cornel rattled in the fkies;

At once tumultuous fhouts and clamours rife.

Nine brothers in a goodly band there ftood,.

Born of Arcadian mix'd with Tufcan blood:

Gylippus' fons : the fatal jav'lin flew,   410

Aim'd at the midmoft of the friendly crew.

A paffage thro' the jointed arms it found,

Juft where the belt was to the body bound;

And ftruck the gentle youth extended on the ground:

Then fir'd with pious rage, the gen'rous train 415

Run madly forward to revenge the flain.

And fome with eager hafte their jav'lins throw;
And fome with fword in hand affault the foe.

   The wifh'd infult the Latin troops embrace;
And meet their ardour in the middle fpace.   420
The Trojans, Tufcans, and Arcadian line,
With equal courage obviate their defign.
Peace leaves the violated fields; and hate
Both armies urges to their mutual fate.
With impious hafte their altars are o'erturn'd, 425
The facrifice half broil'd, and half unburn'd.
Thick ftorms of fteel from either army fly,
And clouds of clafhing darts obfcure the fky:
Brands from the fire, are miffive weapons made:
With chargers, bowls, and all the prieftly trade. 530
Latinus frighted, haftens from the fray,
And bears his unregarded gods away.
Thefe on their horfes vault, thofe yoke the car;
The reft with fwords on high, run headlong to the
                                  [war.

   Meffapus, eager to confound the peace,   435
Spurr'd his hot courfer thro' the fighting prefs,
At king Auleftes; by his purple known
A Tufcan prince, and by his regal crown;
And with a fhock encount'ring, bore him down.

Backward he fell; and as his fate defign'd,   440
The ruins of an altar were behind:
There pitching on his fhoulders, and his head,
Amid the fcatt'ring fires he lay fupinely fpread.
The beamy fpear defcending from above,
His cuirafs pierc'd, and thro' his body drove.   445
Then, with a fcornful fmile, the victor cries;
The gods have found a fitter facrifice.
Greedy of fpoils, th' Italians ftrip the dead
Of his rich armour; and uncrown his head.
　　Prieft Chorinæus arm'd his better hand,   450
From his own altar, with a blazing brand:
And, as Ebufus with a thund'ring pace,
Advanc'd to battle, dafh'd it on his face:
His briftly beard fhines out with fudden fires,
The crackling crop a noifom fcent expires.   455
Following the blow, he feiz'd his curling crown
With his left hand; his other caft him down.
The proftrate body with his knees he prefs'd;
And plung'd his holy poinard in his breaft.
　　While Podalirius, with his fword, purfu'd   460
The fhepherd Alfus thro' the flying crowd,
Swiftly he turns, and aims a deadly blow,
Full on the front of his unwary foe.

The broad axe enters with a craſhing ſound,
And cleavesthechin,withonecontinu'dwound:465
Warm blood, and mingled brains, beſmear his arms
[around.

An iron ſleep his ſtupid eyes oppreſs'd,
And ſeal'd their heavy lids in endleſs reſt.
But good Æneas ruſh'd amid the bands,
Bare was his head, and naked were his hands, 470
In ſign of truce: then thus he cries aloud,
What ſudden rage, what new deſire of blood
Inflames your alter'd minds? O Trojans ceaſe
From impious arms, nor violate the peace.
By human ſanctions, and by laws divine,   475
The terms are all agreed, the war is mine.
Diſmiſs your fears, and let the fight enſue;
This hand alone ſhall right the gods and you:
Our injur'd altars, and their broken vow,
To this avenging ſword the faithleſs Turnus owe.480
     Thus while he ſpoke, unmindful of defence,
A winged arrow ſtruck the pious prince,
But whether from ſome human hand it came,
Or hoſtile god, is left unknown by fame:
No human hand, or hoſtile god was found,   485
To boaſt the triumph of ſo baſe a wound.

When Turnus faw the Trojan quit the plain,
His chiefs difmay'd, his troops a fainting train :
Th' unhop'd event his heighten'd foul infpires,
At once his arms and courfers he requires.   49⦿
Then, with a leap, his lofty chariot gains,
And with a ready hand affumes the reins.
He drives impetuous, and where-e'er he goes,
He leaves behind a lane of flaughter'd foes.
Thefe his lance reaches, over thofe he rolls   495
His rapid car, and crufhes out their fouls :
In vain the vanquifh'd fly ; the victor fends
The dead mens' weapons at their living friends.

   Thus on the banks of Hebrus' freezing flood
The god of battles, in his angry mood,   50⦿
Clafhing his fword againft the brazen fhield,
Lets loofe the reins, and fcours along the field :
Before the wind his fiery courfers fly,
Grones the fad earth, refounds the rattling fky.
Wrath, terror, treafon, tumult, and defpair, 505 ⎫
Dire faces, and deform'd, furround the car ;   ⎬
Friends of the god, and followers of the war.   ⎭

   With fury not unlike, nor lefs difdain,
Exulting Turnus flies along the plain :
His fmoking horfes, at their utmoft fpeed,   51⦿
He lafhes on, and urges o'er the dead.

Their fetlocks run with blood; and when they
{bound,
The gore, and gath'ring duft, are dafh'd around.
Thamyris and Pholus, mafters of the war,
He kill'd at hand, but Sthelenus afar :   515
From far the fons of Imbracus he flew,
Glaucus, and Lades, of the Lycian crew;
Both taught to fight on foot, in battle join'd;
Or mount the courfer that out-ftrips the wind.

Mean time Eumedes, vaunting in the field, 520
New fir'd the Trojans, and their foes repell'd..
This fon of Dolon bore his grandfire's name;
But emulated more his father's fame.
His guileful father, fent a nightly fpy,
The Grecian camp and order to defcry :   525
Hard enterprize, and well he might require
Achilles' carr, and horfes, for his hire;
But, met upon the fcout, th' Etolian prince
In death beftow'd a jufter recompence.

Fierce Turnus view'd the Trojan from afar ; 530
And lanch'd his jav'lin from his lofty carr :
Then lightly leaping down, purfu'd the blow,
And, preffing with his foot, his proftrate foe,
Wrench'd from his feeble hold the fhining fword;
And plung'd it in the bofom of its lord.

Poſſeſs, ſaid he, the fruit of all thy pains,
And meaſure, at thy length, our Latian plains.
Thus are my foes rewarded by my hand,
Thus may they build their town, and thus enjoy the
[land.

Then Daris, Butis, Sybaris he ſlew,   540
Whom o'er his neck the flound'ring courſer threw.
As when loud Boreas with his bluſt'ring train,
Stoops from above, incumbent on the main;
Where-e'er he flies, he drives the rack before;
And rolls the billows on th' Ægean ſhore: 545
So where reſiſtleſs Turnus takes his courſe,
The ſcatter'd ſquadrons bend before his force:
His creſt of horſes hair is blown behind,
By adverſe air, and ruſtles in the wind.

This, haughty Phegeus ſaw with high diſdain, 550
And as the chariot roll'd along the plain,
Light from the ground he leap'd, and ſeiz'd the
[rein.

Thus hung in air, he ſtill retain'd his hold;
The courſers frighted, and their courſe control'd.
The lance of Turnus reach'd him as he hung,   555
And pierc'd his plated arms; but paſs'd along
And only raz'd the ſkin: he turn'd, and held
Againſt his threat'ning foe his ample ſhield;

Then call'd for aid : but while he cry'd in vain,
The chariot bore him backward on the plain.   560
He lies revers'd ; the victor-king defcends,
And ftrikes fo juftly where his helmet ends,
He lops the head.   The Latian fields are drunk,
With ftreams that iffue from the bleeding trunk.

   While he triumphs, and while the Trojans
                                   [yield, 565
The wounded prince is forc'd to leave the field :
Strong Mneftheus, and Achates often try'd,
And young Afcanius weeping by his fide,
Conduct him to his tent : fcarce can he rear
His limbs from earth, fupported on his fpear. 570
Refolv'd in mind, regardlefs of the fmart,
He tugs with both his hands, and breaks the dart.
The fteel remains.   No readier way he found
To draw the weapon, than t' inlarge the wound.
Eager of fight, impatient of delay,   575
He begs ; and his unwilling friends obey.

   Iäpis was at hand to prove his art,
Whofe blooming youth fo fir'd Apollo's heart,
That for his love he proffer'd to beftow
His tuneful harp, and his unerring bow :   580

   Vol. IV   K

The pious youth, more ſtudious how to ſave
His aged ſire, now ſinking to the grave,
Preferr'd the pow'r of plants, and ſilent praiſe
Of healing arts, before Phœbeian bays.

Prop'd on his lance the penſive hero ſtood,   585
And heard, and ſaw unmov'd, the mourning crowd.
The fam'd phyſician tucks his robes around
With ready hands, and haſtens to the wound.
With gentle touches he performs his part,
This way and that, ſoliciting the dart,   590
And exerciſes all his heav'nly art.
All ſoft'ning ſimples, known of ſov'reign uſe,
He preſſes out, and pours their noble juice;
Theſe firſt infus'd, to lenify the pain,
He tugs with pincers, but he tugs in vain.   595
Then to the patron of his art he pray'd;
The patron of his art refus'd his aid.

Mean time the war approaches to the tents:
Th' alarm grows hotter, and the noiſe augments:
The driving duſt proclaims the danger near, 600
And firſt their friends, and then their foes appear;
Their friends retreat, their foes purſue the rear.
The camp is fill'd with terror and affright;
The hiſſing ſhafts within the trench alight;

An undiftinguifh'd noife afcends the fky;   605
The fhouts of thofe who kill, and groans of thofe
                       [who die.
   But now the goddefs mother, mov'd with grief,
And pierc'd with pity, haftens her relief.
A branch of healing Dittany fhe brought,
Which in the Cretan fields with care fhe fought: 610
Rough is the ftem, which woolly leaves furround;
The leaves with flow'rs, the flow'rs with purple
                       [crown'd:
Well known to wounded goats; a fure relief
To draw the pointed fteel, and eafe the grief.
This Venus brings, in clouds involv'd; and brews 615
Th' extracted liquor with Ambrofian dews,
And od'rous Panacee: unfeen fhe ftands,
Temp'ring the mixture with her heav'nly hands:
And pours it in a bowl, already crown'd
With juice of med'c'nal herbs prepar'd to bathe the
                       [wound.
The leech, unknowing of fuperior art,   621 ⎫
Which aids the cure, with this foments the part; ⎬
And in a moment ceas'd the raging fmart.   ⎭
Stanch'd is the blood, and in the bottom ftands:
The fteel, but fcarcely touch'd with tender hands, 625

K 2

Moves up, and follows of its own accord;
And health and vigour are at once reſtor'd.
Iäpis firſt perceiv'd the cloſing wound;
And firſt the footſteps of a god he found.
Arms, arms, he cries, the ſword and ſhield pre-
[pare, 630
And ſend the willing chief, renew'd to war.
This is no mortal work, no cure of mine,
Nor art's effect, but done by hands divine:
Some god our gen'ral to the battle ſends;
Some god preſerves his life for greater ends.   635

 The hero arms in haſt: his hands infold
His thighs with cuiſhes of refulgent gold:
Inflam'd to fight, and ruſhing to the field,
That hand ſuſtaining the cœleſtial ſhield,
This gripes the lance; and with ſuch vigour ſhakes,
That to the reſt the beamy weapon quakes.   641
Then, with a cloſe embrace he ſtrain'd his ſon;
And kiſſing thro' his helmet, thus begun.
My ſon, from my example learn the war,   .⎤
In camps to ſuffer, and in fields to dare: 645⎬
But happier chance than mine attend thy care.   ⎦
This day my hand thy tender age ſhall ſhield,
And crown with honours of the conquer'd field-ı

Thou, when thy riper years shall send thee forth,
To toils of war, be mindful of my worth,   650
Assert thy birthright : and in arms be known,
For Hector's nephew, and Æneas' son.

He said ; and, striding, issu'd on the plain ;
Anteus, and Mnestheus, and a num'rous train
Attend his steps : the rest their weapons take,   655
And crowding to the field, the camp forsake.
A cloud of blinding dust is rais'd around ;
Labours beneath their feet the trembling ground.

Now Turnus, posted on a hill, from far
Beheld the progress of the moving war :   660
With him the Latins view'd the cover'd plains ;
And the chill blood ran backward in their veins.
Juturna saw th' advancing troops appear ;
And heard the hostile sound, and fled for fear.
Æneas leads ; and draws a sweeping train,   665
Clos'd in their ranks, and pouring on the plain.
As when a whirlwind rushing to the shore,
From the mid ocean drives the waves before :
The painful hind, with heavy heart foresees
The flatted fields, and slaughter of the trees ;   670
With such impetuous rage the prince appears,
Before his doubled front ; nor less destruction bears.

K 3

And now both armies fhock, in open field;
Ofyris is by ftrong Thymbræus kill'd.
Archetius, Ufens, Epulon, are flain;   675
(All fam'd in arms, and of the Latian train ;)
By Gyas, Mneftheus, and Achates' hand :
The fatal augur falls, by whofe command
The truce was broken, and whofe lance, embru'd
With Trojan blood, th' unhappy fight renew'd. 680
Loud fhouts and clamours rend the liquid fky;
And o'er the field the frighted Latins fly.
The prince difdains the daftards to purfue,
Nor moves to meet in arms the fighting few :
Turnus alone, amid the dufky plain,   685
He feeks, and to the combat calls in vain.
Juturna heard, and feiz'd with mortal fear,
Forc'd from the beam her brother's charioteer ;.
Affumes his fhape, his armour, and his mien ;
And like Metifcus, in his feat is feen.   690

As the black fwallow near the palace plies ;
O'er empty courts, and under arches flies :
Now hawks aloft, now fkims along the flood,
To furnifh her loquacious neft with food :
So drives the rapid goddefs o'er the plains ;   695
The fmoking horfes run with loofen'd reins.

She steers a various course among the foes ;
Now here, now there, her conqu'ring brother shows :
Now with a straight, now with a wheeling flight,
She turns, and bends, but shuns the single fight. 700
Æneas, fir'd with fury, breaks the croud,
And seeks his foe, and calls by name aloud :
He runs within a narrower ring, and tries
To stop the chariot, but the chariot flies.
If he but gain a glimpse, Juturna fears,   705
And far away the Daunian hero bears.

    What shou'd he do ! nor arts nor arms avail ;
And various cares in vain his mind assail ;
The great Messapus thund'ring thro' the field,
In his left hand two pointed jav'lins held :   710
Encount'ring on the prince, one dart he drew,
And with unerring aim, and utmost vigour threw.
Æneas saw it come, and stooping low
Beneath his buckler, shunn'd the threat'ning blow.
The weapon hiss'd above his head, and tore   715
The waving plume, which on his helm he wore.
Forc'd by this hostile act, and fir'd with spite,
That flying Turnus still declin'd the fight ;
The prince, whose piety had long repell'd
His inborn ardour, now invades the field :   720

Invokes the pow'rs of violated peace,
Their rites, and injur'd altars to redrefs :
Then, to his rage abandoning the rein,
With blood and flaughter'd bodies fills the plain.

What god can tell, what numbers can difplay 725
The various labours of that fatal day ?
What chiefs, and champions fell on either fide,
In combat flain, or by what deaths they dy'd ?
Whom Turnus, whom the Trojan hero kill'd :
Who fhar'd the fame, and fortune of the field ? 730
Jove, cou'dft thou view, and not avert thy fight,⎫
Two jarring nations join'd in cruel fight, ⎬
Who leagues of lafting love fo fhortly fhall unite !⎭

Æneas firft Rutulian Sucro found,
Whofe valour made the Trojans quit the ground :
Betwixt his ribs the jav'lin drove fo juft,   736
It reach'd his heart, nor needs a fecond thruft.
Now Turnus, at two blows, two brethren flew :
Firft from his horfe fierce Amicus he threw ;
Then leaping on the ground, on foot affail'd 740
Diores, and in equal fight prevail'd.
Their lifelefs trunks he leaves upon the place ;
Their heads diftilling gore, his chariot grace.
. Three cold on earth the Trojan hero threw ;
Whom without refpite at one charge he flew : 745

Cethegus, Tanais, Tagus, fell oppress'd,
And sad Onythes, added to the rest;
Of Theban blood, whom Peridia bore.

Turnus, two brothers from the Lycian shore,
And from Apollo's fane to battle sent,   750
O'erthrew, nor Phœbus cou'd their fate prevent.
Peaceful Menætes after these he kill'd,
Who long had shunn'd the dangers of the field:
On Lerna's lake a silent life he led,
And with his nets and angle earn'd his bread. 755
Nor pompous cares, nor palaces he knew,
But wisely from th' infectious world withdrew.
Poor was his house; his father's painful hand
Discharg'd his rent, and plough'd another's land.

As flames among the lofty woods are thrown, 760
On diff'rent sides, and both by winds are blown,
The laurels crackle in the sputt'ring fire;
The frighted silvans from their shades retire:
Or as two neighb'ring torrents fall from high,
Rapid they run; the foamy waters fry: 765
They roll to sea, with unresisted force,
And down the rocks precipitate their course:
Not with less rage the rival heroes take
Their diff'rent ways; nor less destruction make.

K 5

With spears afar, with swords at hand they strike ;
And zeal of slaughter fires their souls alike.
Like them, their dauntless men maintain the field,
And hearts are pierc'd unknowing how to yield :
They blow for blow return, and wound for wound ;
And heaps of bodies raise the level ground.   775
    Murranus, boasting of his blood, that springs
From a long royal race of Latian kings,
Is by the Trojan from his chariot thrown,
Crush'd with the weight of an unwieldy stone :
Betwixt the wheels he fell ; the wheels that bore 780
His living load, his dying body tore.
His starting steeds, to shun the glitt'ring sword,
Paw down his trampled limbs, forgetful of their lord.
    Fierce Hillus threaten'd high ; and face to face
Affronted Turnus in the middle space :   785
The prince encounter'd him in full career,
And at his temples aim'd the deadly spear :
So fatally the flying weapon sped,
That thro' his brazen helm it pierc'd his head.
Nor Cisseus cou'dst thou' scape from Turnus' hand,
In vain the strongest of th' Arcadian band :   791
Nor to Cupentus cou'd his gods afford
Availing aid against th' Ænean sword :

Which to his naked heart purfu'd the courfe:
Nor could his plated fhield fuftain the force.   795
    Iölus fell, whom not the Grecian pow'rs,
Nor great fubverter of the Trojan tow'rs,
Were doom'd to kill, while heav'n prolong'd his date:
But who can pafs the bounds prefix'd by fate;
In high Lyrneſſus, and in Troy, he held   800
Two palaces, and was from each expell'd:
Of all the mighty man, the laſt remains
A little fpot of foreign earth contains.
    And now both hoſts their broken troops unite,
In equal ranks, and mix in mortal fight.   805
Sereſthus, and undaunted Mneſtheus join
The Trojan, Tufcan, and Arcadian line:
Sea-born Meſſapus, with Atinas, heads
The Latin fquadrons, and to battle leads.
They ſtrike, they pufh, they throng the fcanty fpace;
Refolv'd on death, impatient of difgrace;   811
And where one falls, another fills his place.
    The Cyprian goddefs now infpires her fon
To leave the unfiniſhed fight, and ſtorm the town.
For while he rolls his eyes around the plain,   815
In queſt of Turnus, whom he feeks in vain,

He views th' unguarded city from afar,
In carelefs quiet, and fecure of war :
Occafion offers, and excites his mind,
To dare beyond the talk he firft defign'd.   820
Refolv'd, he calls his chiefs ; they leave the fight ;
Attended thus, he takes a neighb'ring height :
The crowding troops about their gen'ral ftand,
All under arms, and wait his high command.
Then thus the lofty prince : Hear and obey : 825
Ye Trojan bands, without the leaft delay.
Jove is with us, and what I have decreed
Requires our utmoft vigour, and our fpeed.
Your inftant arms againft the town prepare ;
The fource of mifchief, and the feat of war, 830
This day the Latian tow'rs, that mate the fky,
Shall level with the plain in afhes lie :
The people fhall be flaves ; unlefs in time
They kneel for pardon, and repent their crime.
Twice have our foes been vanquifh'd on the plain ;
Then fhall I wait till Turnus will be flain ?   836
Your force againft the perjur'd city bend :
There it began, and there the war fhall end.
The peace profan'd our rightful arms requires ;
Cleanfe the polluted place with purging fires.   840

He finifh'd ; and one foul infpiring all,
Form'd in a wedge, the foot approach the wall.
Without the town, an unprovided train
Of gaping, gazing citizens are flain.
Some firebrands, others fcaling ladders bear;   845
And thofe they tofs aloft, and thefe they rear :
The flames now lanch'd, the feather'd arrows fly,
The clouds of miffive arms obfcure the fky.
Advancing to the front, the hero ftands,
And ftretching out to heav'n his pious hands,   850
Attefts the gods, afferts his innocence,
Upbraids with breach of faith th' Aufonian prince :
Declares the royal honour doubly ftain'd,
And twice the rites of holy peace profan'd.

Diffenting clamours in the town arife ;   855
Each will be heard, and all at once advife.
One part for peace, and one for war contends :
Some wou'd exclude their foes, and fome admit their
                                        [friends.
The helplefs king is hurry'd in the throng;
And whate'er tide prevails, is born along.   860
Thus when the fwain, within a hollow rock,
Invades the bees with fuffocating fmoke,
They run around, or labour on their wings,
Difus'd to flight, and fhoot their fleepy ftings;

To fhun the bitter fumes, in vain they try;   865
Black vapours, iffuing from the vent, involve the fky.

    But fate, and envious fortune, now prepare
To plunge the Latins in the laft defpair.
The queen, who faw the foes invade the town ;
And brands on tops of burning houfes thrown; 870
Caft round her eyes, diftracted with her fear ;
No troops of Turnus in the field appear.
Once more fhe ftares abroad, but ftill in vain :
And then concludes the royal youth is flain.
Mad with her anguifh, impotent to bear   875
The mighty grief, fhe loaths the vital air.
She calls herfelf the caufe of all this ill,
And owns the dire effects of her ungovern'd will :
She raves againft the gods, fhe beats her breaft,
She tears with both her hands her purple veft, 880
Then round a beam a running noofe fhe ty'd ;
And, faften'd by the neck, obfcenely dy'd.
  . Soon as the fatal news by Fame was blown,
And to her dames, and to her daughter known ;
The fad Lavinia rends her yellow hair,   885
And rofy cheeks ; the reft her forrow fhare :
With fhrieks the palace rings, and madnefs of
                [defpair.

The fpreading rumour fills the publick place;
Confufion, fear, diftraction, and difgrace,
And filent fhame are feen in ev'ry face.   890

Latinus tears his garments as he goes,
Both for his publick, and his private woes:
With filth his venerable beard befmears,
And fordid duft deforms his filver hairs.
And much he blames the foftnefs of his mind, 895
Obnoxious to the charms of womankind,
And foonreduc'd to change,whathefowelldefign'd:
To break the folemn league fo long defir'd,
Nor finifh what his fates, and thofe of Troy, requir'd.

Now Turnus rolls aloof o'er empty plains, 900
And here and there fome ftraggling foes he gleans.
His flying courfers pleafe him lefs and lefs,
Afham'd of eafy fight, and cheap fuccefs.
Thus half contented, anxious in his mind,
The diftant cries come driving in the wind: 905
Shouts fromthewalls,butfhouts in murmursdrown'd,
A jarring mixture, and a boding found.
Alas, faid he, what mean thefe difmal cries,
What doleful clamours from the town arife?
Confus'd he ftops, and backward pulls the reins: 910
She, who the driver's office now fuftains,

Replies; Neglect, my lord, thefe new alarms;
Here fight, and urge the fortune of your arms:
There want not others to defend the wall:
If by your rival's hand th' Italians fall.   915
So fhall your fatal fword his friends opprefs,
In honour equal, equal in fuccefs.

To this, the prince: O fifter, (for I knew
The peace infring'd, proceeded firft from you,)
I knew you, when you mingled firft in fight, 920
And now in vain you wou'd deceive my fight:
Why, goddefs, this unprofitable care?
Who fent you down from heav'n, involv'd in air?
Your fhare of mortal forrows to fuftain,
And fee your brother bleeding on the plain? 925
For to what pow'r can Turnus have recourfe,
Or how refift his fate's prevailing force!
Thefe eyes beheld Murranus bite the ground,
Mighty the man, and mighty was the wound.
1 heard my deareft friend, with dying breath, 930
My name invoking to revenge his death:
Brave Ufens fell with honour on the place;
To fhun the fhameful fight of my difgrace.
On earth fupine, a manly corpfe he lies;
His veft and armour are the victor's prize.   935

Then shall I see Laurentum in a flame,
Which only wanted to compleat my shame?
How will the Latins hoot their champion's flight;
How Drances will insult, and point them to the fight!
Is death so hard to bear? ye gods below,   940
(Since those above so small compassion show,)
Receive a soul unsully'd yet with shame,
Which not belies my great forefathers' name.

He said: and while he spoke, with flying speed,
Came Sages urging on his foamy steed;   945
Fix'd on his wounded face a shaft he bore,
And seeking Turnus sent his voice before:
Turnus, on you, on you alone depends
Our last relief; compassionate your friends.
Like lightning, fierce Æneas rolling on,   950
With arms invests, with flames invades the town:
The brands are toss'd on high: the winds conspire
To drive along the deluge of the fire:
All eyes are fix'd on you; your foes rejoice;
Ev'n the king staggers, and suspends his choice. 955
Doubts to deliver, or defend the town;
Whom to reject, or whom to call his son.
The queen, on whom your utmost hopes were plac'd,
Herself suborning death, has breath'd her last.

'Tis true, Meſſapus, fearleſs of his fate,   960
With fierce Atinas' aid, defends the gate:
On ev'ry ſide ſurrounded by the foe;
The more they kill, the greater numbers grow;
An iron harveſt mounts, and ſtill remains to mow.
You, far aloof from your forſaken bands,   965
Your rolling chariot drive o'er empty ſands.

Stupid he ſate, his eyes on earth declin'd,
And various cares revolving in his mind:
Rage boiling from the bottom of his breaſt,
And ſorrow mix'd with ſhame,his ſoul oppreſs'd; 970
And conſcious worth lay lab'ring in his thought:
And love by jealouſy to madneſs wrought.
By ſlow degrees his reaſon drove away
The miſts of paſſion, and reſum'd her ſway.
Then, riſing on his car, he turn'd his look;   975
And ſaw the town involv'd in fire and ſmoke.
A wooden tow'r with flames already blaz'd,
Which his own hands on beams and rafters rais'd:
And bridges laid above to join the ſpace:
And wheels below to roll from place to place. 980
Siſter, the fates have vanquiſh'd: let us go
The way which heaven and my hard fortune ſhow.
The fight is fix'd: nor ſhall the branded name
Of a baſe coward blot your brother's fame.

Death is my choice: but fuffer me to try   985
My force, and vent my rage before I die.
He faid, and leaping down without delay,
Thro' crowds of fcatter'd foes he freed his way.
Striding he pafs'd, impetuous as the wind,
And left the grieving goddefs far behind.   990
As when a fragment, from a mountain torn
By raging tempefts, or by torrents born,
Or fapp'd by time, or loofen'd from the roots,
Prone thro' the void the rocky ruin fhoots,
Rolling from crag to crag, from fteep to fteep; 995
Down fink, at once, the fhepherds and their fheep,
Involv'd alike, they rufh to nether ground,
Stun'd with the fhock they fall, and ftun'd from earth
                                        [rebound.:
So Turnus, hafting headlong to the town,
Should'ring and fhoving, bore the fquadrons down.
Still preffing onward, to the walls he drew, 1001
Where fhafts, and fpears, and darts promifcuous
                                        [flew;
And fanguine ftreams the flipp'ry ground embrew.
Firft ftretching out his arm, in fign of peace,
He cries aloud, to make the combat ceafe;   1005
Rutulians, hold, and Latin troops retire;
The fight is mine, and me the gods require.

'Tis juft that I fhou'd vindicate alone
The broken truce, or for the breach atone.
This day fhall free from wars th'Aufonian ftate; 1010
Or finifh my misfortunes in my fate.

Both armies from their bloody work defift :
And, bearing backward, form a fpacious lift.
The Trojan hero, who receiv'd from fame   1014
The welcome found, and heard the champion's name,
Soon leaves the taken works, and mounted walls,
Greedy of war, where greater glory calls.
He fprings to fight, exulting in his force ;
His jointed armour rattles in the courfe.
Like Eryx, or like Athos, great he fhows,   1020
Or father Appenine, when white with fnows,
His head divine, obfcure in clouds he hides,
And fhakes the founding foreft on his fides.

The nations over-'aw'd, furceafe the fight,
Immoveable their bodies, fix'd their fight :   1025
Ev'n Death ftands ftill; nor from above they throw
Their darts, nor drive their batt'ring-rams below.
In filent order either army ftands ;
And drop their fwords, unknowing, from their hands.
Th'Aufoniankingbeholds, withwond'ringfight, 1030
Two mighty champions match'd in fingle fight ;

Born under climes remote; and brought by fate,
With swords to try their titles to the state.

Now in clos'd field, each other from afar
They view; and rushing on, begin the war.   1035
They lanch their spears, then hand to hand they meet;
The trembling soil resounds beneath their feet :
Their bucklers clash ; thick blows descend from high,
And flakes of fire from their hard helmets fly.
Courage conspires with chance; and both engage 1040
With equal fortune yet, and mutual rage.

As when two bulls for their fair female fight,
In Sila's shades, or on Taburnus' height ;
With horns adverse they meet : the keeper flies :
Mute stands the herd, the heifers roll their eyes ; 1045
And wait th' event; which victor they shall bear,
And who shall be the lord, to rule the lusty year :
With rage of love the jealous rivals burn,
And push for push, and wound for wound return :
Their dewlaps gor'd, their sides are lav'd in blood : 1050
Loud cries and roaring sounds rebellow thro' the wood :
Such was the combat in the listed ground ;
So clash their swords, and so their shields resound.

Jove sets the beam ; in either scale he lays
The champion's fate, and each exactly weighs. 1055

On this fide life, and lucky chance afcends :

Loaded with death, that other fcale defcends.

Rais'd on the ftretch, young Turnus aims a blow,

Full on the helm of his unguarded foe :

Shrill fhouts and clamours ring on either fide : 1060

As hopes and fears their panting hearts divide.

But all in pieces flies the traitor fword,

And, in the middle ftroke, deferts his lord.

Now 'tis but death, or flight : difarm'd he flies,

When in his hand, an unknown hilt he fpies. 1065

Fame fays that Turnus, when his fteeds he join'd,⎫

Hurrying to war, diforder'd in his mind,   ⎬

Snatch'd the firft weapon, which his hafte cou'd find.⎭

'Twas not the fated fword his father bore ;

But that his charioteer Metifcus wore.   1070

This, while the Trojans fled, the toughnefs held :

But vain againft the great Vulcanian fhield.

The mortal-temper'd fteel deceiv'd his hand :

The fhiver'd fragments fhone amid the fand.

Surpriz'd with fear, he fled along the field ; 1075

And now forthright, and now in orbits wheel'd.

For here the Trojan troops the lift furround ;

And there the pafs is clos'd with pools of marfhy

[ground.

Æneas haftens; tho' with heavier pace,
His wound, fo newly knit, retards the chafe: 1080
And oft his trembling knees their aid refufe,
Yet preffing foot by foot his foe purfues.

   Thus, when a fearful ftag is clos'd around
With crimfon toils, or in a river found;
High on the bank the deep-mouth'd hound appears;
Stillopening,followingftill,where-e'er hefteers: 1086
The perfecuted creature to and fro,
Turns here and there to 'fcape his Umbrian foe:
Steep is th' afcent, and if he gains the land,
The purple death is pitch'd along the ftrand: 1090
His eager foe determin'd to the chace,
Stretch'd at his length gains ground at ev'ry pace:
Now to his beamy head he makes his way,
And now he holds, or thinks he holds his prey:
Juft at the pinch the ftag fprings out with fear, 1095
He bites the wind, and fills his founding jaws with air.
The rocks, the lakes, the meadows ring with cries;
The mortal tumult mounts, and thunders in thefkies.

   Thus flies the Daunian prince: and, flying, blames
His tardy troops; and calling by their names, 1100
Demands his trufty fword.   The Trojan threats
The realm with ruin, and their ancient feats

To lay in afhes, if they dare fupply

With arms or aid, his vanquifh'd enemy :

Thus menacing, he ftill purfues the courfe, 1105

With vigour, tho' diminifh'd of his force.

Ten times already, round the lifted place,

One chief had fled, and t'other giv'n the chace :

No trivial prize is play'd ; for on the life

Or death of Turnus, now depends the ftrife. 1110

Within the fpace, an olive tree had ftood, ·

A facred fhade, a venerable wood,

For vows to Faunus paid, the Latins guardian god.

Here hung the vefts, and tablets were ingrav'd,

Of finking mariners from fhipwreck fav'd.   1115

With heedlefs hands the Trojans fell'd the tree,

To make the ground inclos'd for combat free.

Deep in the root, whether by fate or chance,

Or erring hafte, the Trojan drove his lance; 1119

Then ftoop'd, and tugg'd with force immenfe, to free

Th' incumber'd fpear from the tenacious tree ;

That whom his fainting limbs purfu'd in vain,

His flying weapon might from far attain.

Confus'd with fear, bereft of human aid,   1124

Then Turnus to the gods, and firft to Faunus pray'd.

O Faunus pity, and thou mother earth,

Where I thy fofter fon receiv'd my birth,

Hold faſt the ſteel ; if my religious hand
Your plant has honour'd, which your foes profan'd ;
Propitious hear my pious pray'r ! He ſaid,   1130
Nor with ſuccefslefs vows invok'd their aid.
Th' incumbent hero wrench'd, and pull'd, and ſtrain'd
But ſtill the ſtubborn earth the ſteel detain'd.
Juturna took her time : and while in vain
He ſtrove, aſſum'd Metiſcus' form again :   1135
And, in that imitated ſhape, reſtor'd
To the deſpairing prince, his Daunian ſword.
The queen of love, who with diſdain and grief,
Saw the bold nymph afford this prompt relief ;
T' aſſert her offspring with a greater deed,   1140
From the tough root the ling'ring weapon freed.

   Once more erect, the rival chiefs advance ;
One truſts the ſword, and one the pointed lance :
And both reſolv'd alike, to try the fatal chance.

   Mean time imperial Jove to Juno ſpoke,   1145
Who from a ſhining cloud beheld the ſhock :
What new arreſt, O queen of heav'n, is ſent
To ſtop the fates now lab'ring in th' event ?
What further hopes are left thee to purſue ?
Divine Æneas, (and thou know'ſt it too,)   1150
Free-dom'd to theſe celeſtial ſeats is due.

   Vol. IV.   L

What more attempts for Turnus can be made,
That thus thou ling'reſt in this lonely ſhade!
Is it becoming of the due reſpect,
And awful honour of a god elect,   1155
A wound unworthy of our ſtate to feel;
Patient of human hands, and earthly ſteel?
Or ſeems it juſt, the ſiſter ſhould reſtore
A ſecond ſword, when one was loſt before; 1159
And arm a conquer'd wretch, againſt his conqueror?

For what without thy knowledge and avow,
Nay more, thy dictate, doſt Juturna do?
At laſt, in deference to my love, forbear
To lodge within thy ſoul this anxious care:
Reclin'd upon my breaſt, thy grief unload; 1165
Who ſhould relive the goddeſs but the god?
Now, all things to their utmoſt iſſue tend;
Puſh'd by the fates to their appointed end:
While leave was giv'n thee, and a lawful hour
For vengeance, wrath, and unreſiſted pow'r: 1170
Toſs'd on the ſeas thou cou'dſt thy foes diſtreſs,
And driv'n aſhore, with hoſtile arms oppreſs:
Deform the royal houſe; and from the ſide
Of the juſt bridegroom, tear the plighted bride:

Now ceaſe at my command. The Thund'rer ſaid:
And with dejected eyes this anſwer Juno made. 1176

Becaufe your dread decree too well I knew;
From Turnus and from earth unwilling I withdrew,
Elfe fhou'd you not behold me here alone,
Involv'd in empty clouds my friends bemoan; 1180
But girt with vengeful flames, in open fight,
Engag'd againft my foes in mortal fight.
'Tis true, Juturna mingled in the ftrife
By my command, to fave her brother's life;
At leaft to try: but by the Stygian lake,   1185
(The moft religious oath the gods can take,)
With this reftriction, not to bend the bow,
Or tofs the fpear, or trembling dart to throw.
And now refign'd to your fuperior might,
And tir'd with fruitlefs toils, I loath the fight. 1190
This let me beg, (and this no fates withftand)
Both for myfelf, and for your father's land;
That when the nuptial bed fhall bind the peace,
(Which I, fince you ordain, confent to blefs,)
The laws of either nation be the fame;   1195
But let the Latins ftill retain their name;
Speak the fame language which they fpoke before;
Wear the fame habits which their grandfires wore:
Call them not Trojans: perifh the renown,
And name of Troy with that detefted town. 1200

L 2

Latium be Latium ftill ; let Alba reign, .
And Rome's immortal majefty remain.

   Then thus the founder of mankind replies,
(Unruffled was his front, ferene his eyes.)
Can Saturn's iffue, and heav'n's other heir,   1205
Such endlefs anger in her bofom bear ? .
Be miftrefs, and your full defires obtain :
But quench the choler you foment in vain.
From ancient blood th'Aufonian people fprung, 12c9
Shall keep their name, their habit, and their tongue.
The Trojans to their cuftoms fhall be ty'd, ⎫
I will, myfelf, their common rites provide ; ⎬
The native fhall command, the foreigners fubfide. ⎭
All fhall be Latium ; Troy without a name :
And her loft fons forget from whence they came. 1215
From blood fo mix'd, a pious race fhall flow, .
Equal to gods, excelling all below.
No nation more refpect to you fhall pay,
Or greater off'rings on your altars lay.
Juno confents, well pleas'd that her defires   1220
Had found fuccefs, and from the cloud retires.

   The peace thus made, the Thund'rer next prepares
To force the wat'ry goddefs from the wars.
Deep in the difmal regions, void of light,
Three daughters at a birth were born to night : 1225

Thefe their brown mother, brooding on her care, ⎫
Indulg'd with windy wings to flit in air :   ⎬
With ferpents girt alike ; and crown'd with hiffing ⎪
                                [hair. ⎭

In heav'n the Diræ call'd, and ftill at hand,
Before the throne of angry Jove they ftand,   1230
His minifters of wrath ; and ready ftill
The minds of mortal men with fears to fill :
When-e'er the moody fire, to wreak his hate
On realms or towns, deferving of their fate,
Hurls down difeafes, death and deadly care,   1235
And terrifies the guilty world with war.
One fifter-plague of thefe from heav'n he fent,
To fright Juturna with a dire portent.
The peft comes whirling down : by far more flow
Springs the fwift arrow from the Parthian bow,   1240
Or Cydon eugh ; when traverfing the fkies,
And drench'd in pois'nous juice, the fure deftruction
                                 flies·

With fuch a fudden, and unfeen a flight,
Shot thro' the clouds the daughter of the night.
Soon as the field inclos'd fhe had in view,   1245
And from afar her deftin'd quarry knew :

L 3

Contracted, to the boding bird she turns,
Which hunts the ruin'd piles, and hallow'd urns,
And beats about the tombs with nightly wings;
Where songs obscene on sepulchres she sings. 1250
Thus lessen'd in her form, with frightful cries ⎫
The fury round unhappy Turnus flies,   ⎬
Flaps on his shield, and flutters o'er his eyes. ⎭
A lazy chilness crept along his blood,
Chok'd was his voice, his hair with horror stood. 1255
Juturna from afar beheld her fly,
And knew th' ill omen, by her screaming cry,
And stridour of her wing. Amaz'd with fear,
Her beauteous breasts she beat, and rent her flowing
                                   [hair.
Ah me, she cries, in this unequal strife,   1260
What can thy sister more to save thy life!
Weak as I am, can I, alas, contend
In arms, with that inexorable fiend!
Now, now, I quit the field! forbear to fright
My tender soul, ye baleful birds of night!   1265
The lashing of your wings I know too well:
The founding flight, and fun'ral screams of hell!
These are the gifts you bring from haughty Jove,
The worthy recompence of ravish'd love!

Did he for this exempt my life from fate?   1270
O hard conditions of immortal state!
Tho' born to death, not privileg'd to die,
But forc'd to bear impos'd eternity!
Take back your envious bribes, and let me go
Companion to my brother's ghost below!   2275
The joys are vanish'd: nothing now remains
Of life immortal, but immortal pains.
What earth will open her devouring womb,
To rest a weary goddess in the tomb!
She drew a length of sighs; nor more she said,   1280
But in her azure mantle wrap'd her head:
Then plung'd into her stream, with deep despair,
And her last sobs came bubbling up in air.

　　Now stern Æneas waves his weighty spear
Against his foe, and thus upbraids his fear: 1285
What farther subterfuge can Turnus find?
What empty hopes are harbour'd in his mind?
'Tis not thy swiftness can secure thy flight:
Not with their feet, but hands, the valiant fight.
Vary thy shape in thousand forms, and dare   1290
What skill and courage can attempt in war:

L 4

Wifh for the wings of wind to mount the fky ;
Or hid, within the hollow earth to lie.
The champion fhook his head; and made this fhort
[reply.

No threats of thine, my manly mind can move : 1295
'Tis hoftile heav'n I dread ; and partial Jove.
He faid no more ; but with a figh, reprefs'd
The mighty forrow, in his fwelling breaft.
Then, as he roll'd his troubled eyes around,
An antique ftone he faw; the common bound 1300
Of neighb'ring fields ; and barrier of the ground :
So vaft, that twelve ftrong men of modern days,
Th' enormous weight from earth cou'd hardly raife.
He heav'd it at a lift : and pois'd on high,
Ran ftagg'ring on, againft his enemy.   1305
But fo diforder'd, that he fcarcely knew
His way : or what unwieldy weight he threw.
His knocking knees are bent beneath the load :
And fhiv'ring cold congeals his vital blood.
The ftone drops from his arms ; and falling fhort,
For want of vigour, mocks his vain effort.   1311
And as, when heavy fleep has clos'd the fight,
The fickly fancy labours in the night :
We feem to run ; and, deftitute of force,
Our finking limbs forfake us in the courfe :   1315

In vain we heave for breath; in vain we cry :
The nerves unbrac'd, their usual strength deny;
And on the tongue the falt'ring accents die :
So Turnus far'd, whatever means he try'd,
All force of arms, and points of art employ'd, 1320
The fury flew athwart, and made th' endeavour
　　　　　　　　　　　　　　　　[void.]

A thousand various thoughts his soul confound :
He star'd about; nor aid nor issue found :
His own men stop the pass; and his own walls
　　　　　　　　　　　　　　　　[surround.]

Once more he pauses; and looks out again : 1325
And seeks the goddess charioteer in vain.
Trembling he views the thund'ring chief advance,
And brandishing aloft the deadly lance :
Amaz'd he cow'rs beneath his conq'ring foe,
Forgets to ward; and waits the coming blow. 1330
Astonish'd while he stands, and fix'd with fear,
Aim'd at his shield he sees th' impending spear.

The hero measur'd first, with narrow view,
The destin'd mark : and rising as he threw,
With its full swing the fatal weapon flew. 1335
Not with less rage the rattling thunder falls;
Or stones from batt'ring engines break the walls :

Swift as a whirlwind, from an arm so strong,
The lance drove on; and bore the death along.
Nought cou'd his sev'n-fold shield the prince avail;
Nor ought beneath his arms the coat of mail;　1341
It pierc'd thro' all; and with a grizly wound,
Transfix'd his thigh; and doubled him to ground.
With groans the Latins rend the vaulted sky:
Woods, hills, and valleys, to the voice reply.　1345
: Now low on earth the lofty chief is laid,
With eyes cast upwards, and with arms display'd; ⎫
And recreant thus to the proud victor pray'd.　⎭
I know my death deserv'd, nor hope to live:
Use what the gods, and thy good fortune give.　1350
　Yet think; oh think, if mercy may be shown,
(Thou hadst a father once; and hast a son:)
Pity my sire, now sinking to the grave;
And for Anchises' sake, old Daunus save!
Or, if thy vow'd revenge pursue my death;　1355
Give to my friends my body void of breath!
The Latian chiefs have seen me beg my life; ⎫
Thine is the conquest, thine the royal wife; ⎬
Against a yielded man, 'tis mean ignoble strife.　⎭
　In deep suspence the Trojan seem'd to stand;　1360
And, just prepar'd to strike, repress'd his hand.

He roll'd his eyes, and ev'ry moment felt
His manly foul with more compaffion melt.
When, cafting down a cafual glance he fpy'd
The golden belt that glitter'd on his fide :   1365
The fatal fpoils which haughty Turnus tore
From dying Pallas, and in triumph wore.
Then rouz'd anew to wrath, he loudly cries
(Flames, while he fpoke, cameflafhingfrom his eyes :)
Traitor, doft thou, doft thou to grace pretend, 1370
Clad, as thou art, in trophies of my friend ?
To his fad foul a grateful off'ring go ;
'Tis Pallas, Pallas gives this deadly blow.
He rais'd his arm aloft ; and at the word,
Deep in his bofom drove the fhining fword.   1375
The ftreaming blood diftain'd his arms around,
And the difdainful foul came rufhing thro' the
                                        [wound.

L 6

POSTSCRIPT

TO THE

READER.

WHAT Virgil wrote in the vigour of his age, in plenty and at eafe, I have undertaken to *tranflate* in my declineing years: ftruggling with wants, oppreffed with ficknefs, curbed in my genius, liable to be mifconftrued in all I write; and my judges, if they are not very equitable, already prejudiced againft me, by the *lying character* which has been given them of my morals. Yet fteady to my principles, and not difpirited with my afflictions, I have, by the bleffing of God on my endeavours, overcome all difficulties; and, in fome meafure, acquitted myfelf of the debt which I owed the public, when I undertook this work. In the firft place therefore, I thankfully acknowledge to the Almighty Power, the affiftance he has given me in the beginning, the profecution, and *conclufion* of my prefent ftudies, which are more happily performed, than I could have promifed to myfelf, when I laboured under fuch difcouragements. For, what I have done, imperfect as it is, for want of health and leifure to correct it, will be judged in afterages, and poffibly in the prefent, to be no difhonour to my native country; whofe language and poetry would be more efteemed abroad, if they were better underftood. Somewhat (give me leave to fay) I have added to both of them in the choice of *words*, and harmony of numbers, which were wanting, efpecially the laft, in all our poets, even in thofe who being endued with genius, yet have not cultivated their mother-tongue with fufficient care; or relying on the beauty of their thoughts, have judged the ornament of words, and fweetnefs of found, unneceffary. One is for raking in Chaucer (our Englifh Ennius) for antiquated words, which are never to be revived, but when found or fignificancy is wanting in the prefent language. But many of his deferve not this redemption, any more than the crowds of men who daily die, or are flain for fix-pence in a battle, merit to be reftored to life, if a wifh could revive them. Others have no ear for verfe, nor choice of words; nor diftinction of thoughts; but mingle farthings with their gold to make up the fum. Here is a field of fatire opened to me: but fince the revolution, I have wholly renounced that talent. For who would give phyfick to the great, when he is uncalled? to do his patient no good, and endanger himfelf for his prefcription? Neither am I ignorant, but I may juftly be condemned for many of thofe faults, of which I have too liberally arraigned others.

Cynthius aurem vellit, & admonuit.

It is enough for me, if the government will let me pafs unqueftioned. In the mean time, I am obliged in gratitude to return my thanks to many of them, who have not only diftinguifhed me from others of the fame party, by a particular exception of grace, but without confidering the man, have been bountiful to the poet: have encouraged Virgil to fpeak fuch Englifh, as I could teach him, and reward his interpreter, for the pains he has taken in bringing him over into Britain, by defraying the charges of his voyage. Even Cerberus,

when he had received the fop, permitted
Æneas to pafs freely to Elyfium. Had it
been offered me, and I had refufed it, yet
ftill fome gratitude is due to fuch who were
willing to oblige me. But how much more
to thofe from whom I have received the
favours which they have offered to one of a
different perfuafion? amongft whom I cannot omit naming the earls of Derby and of
Peterborough. To the firft of thefe, I have
not the honour to be known ; and therefore
his liberality was as much unexpected, as it
was undeferved. The prefent earl of Peterborough has been pleafed long fince to accept
the tenders of my fervice : his favours are
fo frequent to me, that I receive them almoft
by prefcription. No difference of interefts
or opinion have been able to withdraw his
protection from me : and I might juftly
be condemned for the moft unthankful of
mankind, if I did not always preferve for
him a moft profound refpect and inviolable
gratitude. I muft alfo add, that if the laft
Æneid fhine among its fellows, it is owing
to the commands of Sir William Trumball,
one of the principal fecretaries of ftate,
who recommended it, as his favourite, to
my care ; and for his fake particularly I
have made it mine. For who would confefs
wearinefs, when he enjoined a frefh labour?

I could not but invoke the affiftance of a mufe, for this laft office.

Extremum hunc Arethufa : ——
Negat quis carmina Gallo ?

Neither am I to forget the noble prefent which was made me by Gilbert Dolben, Efq. the worthy fon of the late archbifhop of York : who, when I began this work, enriched me with all the feveral editions of Virgil, and all the commentaries of thofe editions in Latin. Amongft which, I could not but prefer the Dauphine's, as the laft, the fhorteft, and the moft judicious. Fabrini I had alfo fent me from Italy ; but either he underftands Virgil but very imperfectly, or I have no knowledge of my author.

Being invited by that worthy Gentleman Sir William Bowyer, to Denham-Court, I tranflated the firft Georgic at his houfe, and the greateft part of the laft Æneid. A more friendly entertainment no man ever found. No wonder therefore if both thofe verfions furpafs the reft, and own the fatisfaction I received in his converfe, with whom I had the honour to be bred in Cambridge, and in the fame college. The feventh Æneid was made Englifh at Burleigh, the magnificent abode of the Earl of Exeter : in a village belonging to his family I was born, and

under his roof I endeavoured to make that
Æneid appear in English with as much lustre
as I could: though my author has not
given the finishing strokes either to it or
to the eleventh, as I perhaps could prove
in both, if I durst presume to criticize my
master.

By a letter from William Walsh of Abber-
ly, Esq. (who has so long honoured me with
his friendship, and who, without flattery, is
the best critick of our nation) I have been
informed that his Grace the Duke of Shrews-
bury has procured a printed copy of the
Pastorals, Georgics, and six first Æneids, from
my bookseller, and has read them in the
country, together with my friend. This
noble person having been pleased to give
them a commendation, which I presume not
to insert; has made me vain enough to boast
of so great a favour, and to think I have
succeeded beyond my hopes; the character
of his excellent judgment, the acuteness of
his wit, and his general knowledge of good
letters, being known as well to all the world,
as the sweetness of his disposition, his hu-
manity, his easiness of access, and desire of
obliging those who stand in need of his
protection, are known to all who have ap-
proached him; and to me in particular,
who have formerly had the honour of his
conversation. Whoever has given the world

J. Colper sculp.

the tranflation of part of the third Georgic, which he calls *The Power of Love*, has put me to fufficient pains to make my own not inferior to his: as my Lord Rofcommon's Silenus had formerly given me the fame trouble. The moft ingenious Mr. Addifon of Oxford has alfo been as troublefome to me as the other two, and on the fame account. After his bees, my latter fwarm is fcarcely worth the hiving. Mr. Cowley's *Praife of a Country Life* is excellent; but is rather an imitation of Virgil, than a verfion. That I have recovered in fome meafure the health which I had loft by too much application to this work, is owing, next to God's mercy, to the fkill and care of Dr. Guibbons, and Dr. Hobbs, the two ornaments of their profeffion; whom I can only pay by this acknowledgement. The whole faculty has always been ready to oblige me; and the only one of them, who endeavoured to defame me, had it not in his power.*
I defire pardon for my readers for faying fo much in relation to myfelf, which concerns not them: and with my acknowledgements to all my fubfcribers, have only to add, that the few notes which follow, are *par maniere d'acquit*, becaufe I had obliged myfelf by articles to do fomewhat of that

* Sir Richard Blackmore.

kind. Thefe fcattering obfervations are rather gueffes at my author's meaning in fome paffages, than proofs that fo he meant. The unlearned may have recourfe to any poetical dictionary in Englifh, for the names of perfons, places, or fables, which the learned need not: but that little which I fay, is either new or neceffary. And the firft of thefe qualifications never fails to invite a reader, if not to pleafe him.

Notes *and* Obfervations

O N

VIRGIL's WORKS

I N

ENGLISH.

PASTORAL 1. Line 6. *There firft the youth of heavenly birth I viewed.*

Virgil means Octavius Cæfar, heir to Julius; who perhaps had not arrived to his twentieth year, when Virgil faw him firft. *Vide* his life. Of heavenly birth or heavenly blood; becaufe the Julian family was derived from Iülus, fon to Æneas, and grandfon to Venus.

Paftoral 2. Line 65. *The fhort Narciffus.* That is, of fhort continuance.

Paſtoral 3.   Line 95. *For him, the god of ſhep-herds and their ſheep.*

Phœbus, not Pan, is here called the god of ſhep-herds: the poet alludes to the ſame ſtory, which he touches in the beginning of the ſecond Georgic, where he calls Phœbus the Amphryſian ſhepherd, becauſe he fed the ſheep and oxen of Admetus (with whom he was in love) on the hill Amphryſus.

Paſtoral 4.   Line 73. *Begin auſpicious boy,* &c. In Latin thus, *Incipe parve puer, riſu cognoſcere ma-trem,* &c.

I have tranſlated the paſſage to this ſenſe; that the infant ſmiling on his mother, ſingles her out from the reſt of the company about him.   Erythræus, Bembus, and Joſeph Scaliger, are of this opinion. Yet they and I may be miſtaken.   For immediately after, we find theſe words, *Cui non riſere Parentes,* which imply another ſenſe, as if the parents ſmiled on the new-born infant: and that the babe on whom they vouchſafed not to ſmile, was born to ill-fortune. For they tell a ſtory, that when Vulcan, the only ſon of Jupiter and Juno, came into the world, he was ſo hard-favoured, that both his parents frowned on him; and Jupiter threw him out of heaven: he fell on the iſland Lemnos, and was lame ever after-wards.   The laſt line of the paſtoral ſeems to juſtify this ſenſe, *Nec deus hunc Menſâ, Dea nec dignata Cubili eſt.*   For though he married Venus, yet his mother Juno was not preſent at the nuptials to bleſs them; as appears by his wife's incontinence.   They

fay alfo, that he was banifhed from the banquets of
the gods : if fo, that punifhment could be of no
long continuance, for Homer makes him prefent at
their feafts ; and compofing a quarrel betwixt his
parents, with a bowl of nectar.   The matter is of
no great confequence ; and therefore I adhere to my
tranflation, for thefe two reafons : firft, Virgil has
this following line, *Matri longa decemtulerunt faftidia
menfes,* as if the infant's fmiling on his mother,
was a reward to her for bearing him ten months in
her body, four weeks longer than the ufual time.
Secondly, Catullus is cited by Jofeph Scaliger, as
favouring this opinion, in his Epithalamium of
Manlius Torquatus.

> *Torquatus, volo parvolus*
> *Matris è gremio fuæ*
> *Porrigens teneras manus*
> *Dulcè rideat ad Patrem,* &c.

What if I fhould fteer betwixt the two extremes,
and conclude, that the infant, who was to be happy,
muft not only fmile on his parents, but alfo they on
him ? for Scaliger notes that the infants who fmiled
not at their birth, were obferved to be Ἀγίλαςοι, or
fullen (as I have tranflated it) during all their
life : and Servius, and almoft all the modern commentators affirm, that no child was thought for-
tunate on whom his parents fmiled not at his birth.
I obferve farther, that the ancients thought the infant who came into the world at the end of the tenth
month, was born to fome extraordinary fortune,

good or bad. Such was the birth of the late prince of Conde's father, of whom his mother was not brought to bed, till almoſt eleven months were expired after his father's death : yet the College of Phyſicians at Paris, concluded he was lawfully begotten. My ingenious friend, Anthony Henley, Eſq. deſired me to make a note on this paſſage of Virgil : adding, what I had not read; that the Jews have been ſo ſuperſtitious, as to obſerve not only the firſt look or action of an infant, but alſo the firſt word which the parent or any of the aſſiſtants ſpoke after the birth : and from thence they gave a name to the child alluding to it.

Paſtoral 6. My Lord Roſcommon's notes on this paſtoral, are equal to his excellent tranſlation of it; and thither I refer the reader.

The eighth and tenth Paſtorals are already tranſlated to all manner of advantage, by my excellent friend Mr. Stafford. So is the Epiſode of Camilla, in the eleventh Æneid.

This eighth Paſtoral is copied by our author from two Bucolicks of Theocritus. Spencer has followed both Virgil and Theocritus, in the charms which he employs for curing Britomartis of her love. But he had alſo our poet's Ceiris in his eye : for there not only the inchantments are to be found : but alſo the very name of Britomartis.

In the ninth Paſtoral, Virgil has made a collection of many ſcattering paſſages, which he had tranſlated from Theocritus : and here he has bound them into a noſegay.

Georgic 1. The poetry of this book is more fublime than any part of Virgil, if I have any tafte. And if ever I have copied his majeftick ftyle, it is here. The compliment he makes Auguftus almoft in the beginning, is ill imitated by his fucceffors Lucan and Statius. They dedicated to tyrants; and their flatteries are grofs and fulfom. Virgil's addrefs is both more lofty and more juft. In the three laft lines' of this Georgic, I think I have difcovered a fecret compliment to the Emperor, which none of the commentators have obferved. Virgil had juft before defcribed the miferies which Rome had undergone betwixt the Triumvirs and the Common-wealth party: in the clofe of all, he feems to excufe the crimes committed by his patron Cæfar, as if he were conftrained againft his own temper to thofe violent proccedings, by the neceffity of the times in general, but more particularly by his two partners, Anthony and Lepidus. *Fertur Equis Auriga, nec audit Currus habenas.* They were the head-ftrong horfes, who hurried Octavius, the trembling charioteer, along, and were deaf to his reclaiming them. I obferve farther; that the prefent wars, in which all Europe, and part of Afia are engaged at prefent, are waged in the fame places here defcribed; *Atque hinc Euphrates, illinc Germania bellum,* &c. As if Virgil had prophefied of this age.

Georgic 2. The praifes of Italy, (tranflated by the learned, and every way excellent Mr. Chetwood, which are printed in one of my mifcellany poems) are the greateft ornament of this book. Wherein

for want of fufficient fkill in gardening, agriculture, &c. I may poffibly be miftaken in fome
terms. But concerning grafting, my honoured
friend Sir William Bowyer has affured me, that
Virgil has fhewn more of poetry than fkill, at leaft
in relation to our more northern climates. And
that many of our ftocks will not receive fuch grafts,
as our poet tells us would bear in Italy. Nature
has confpired with art to make the garden at Denham-court, of Sir William's own plantation, one
of the moft delicious fpots of ground in England :
it contains not above five acres, (juft the compafs of
Alcinous his garden, defcribed in the Odyffes :) But
Virgil fays in this very Georgic, *Laudato ingentia
rura; exiguum colito.*

Georgic 3.   Line 45.
Next him Niphates, with inverted urn, &c.

It has been objected to me, that I underftood not
this paffage of Virgil, becaufe I call Niphates a river,
which is a mountain in Armenia. But the river,
arifing from the fame mountain is alfo called Niphates. And having fpoken of Nile before, I might
reafonably think, that Virgil rather meant to couple
two rivers, than a river and a mountain.

Line 224.   *The male has done, &c.*

The tranfition is obfcure in Virgil. He began
with cows, then proceeds to treat of horfes; now
returns to cows.

Line 476. *Till the new ram receives th' exalted sun.*

Astrologers tell us, that the sun receives his exaltation in the sign Aries : Virgil perfectly understood both Astronomy and Astrology.

Georgic 4. Line 27. *That when the youthful prince.*

My most ingenious friend Sir Henry Shere, has observed through a glass hive, that the young prince of the *Bees,* or heir presumptive of the crown, approaches the king's apartment with great reverence ; and for three successive mornings demands permission to lead forth a colony of that year's bees. If his petition be granted, which he seems to make by humble hummings ; the swarm arises under his conduct : if the answer be, *le roy s'avisera,* that is, if the old monarch think it not convenient for the publick good, to part with so many of his subjects; the next morning the prince is found dead, before the threshold of the palace.

Line 477.   The poet here records the names of fifty river-nymphs.   And for once I have translated them all.   But in the Æneis I thought not myself obliged to be so exact : for in naming many men who were killed by heroes, I have omitted some, which would not sound in English verse.

Line 660.   The Episode of Orpheus and Euridice begins here, and contains the only machine which Virgil uses in the Georgics.   I have observed in the epistle before the Æneis, that our Author seldom employs machines but to adorn his *poem :* and that the action which they seemingly perform, is

really produced without them. Of this nature is the
legend of the bees reftored by miracle; when the
receipt which the poet gives, would do the work
without one.   The only beautiful machine which I
remember in the modern poets, is in Ariofto; where
God commands St. Michael to take care, that Paris,
then befieged by the Saracens, fhould be fuccoured
by Rinaldo.   In order to this, he enjoins the arch-
angel to find Silence and Difcord.   The firft to conduct the Chriftian army to relieve the town, with fo
much fecrefy, that their march fhould not be difcovered; the latter to enter the camp of the infidels,
and there to fow diffention among the principal commanders.   The heavenly meffenger takes his way to
an ancient monaftery; not doubting there to find
Silence in her primitive abode; but inftead of Silence
finds Difcord; the Monks, being divided into factions, about the choice of fome new officer, were at
fnic and *fnee* with their drawn knives.   The fatire
needs no explanation.   And here it may be alfo obferved, that ambition, jealoufy, and worldly intereft,
and point of honour, had made variance both in the
cloifter and the camp; and ftrict difcipline had done
the work of Silence, in conducting the Chriftian
army to furprife the Turks.

Æneid 1. Line 111.
And make thee father of a happy line.

This was an obliging promife to Æolus; who
had been fo unhappy in his former children Maca-
reus and Canace.

: Line 196. *The realms of ocean, and the fields of air are mine, not his.*

Poetically fpeaking, the *fields of air* are under the command of Juno ; and her vicegerent Æolus. Why then does Neptune call them his ? I anfwer, becaufe being god of the feas, Æolus could raife no tempeft in the atmofphere above them without his leave. But why does Juno addrefs to her own fub-ftitute ? I anfwer, He had an immediate power over the winds, whom Juno defires to employ on her revenge.   That power was abfolute by land ; which Virgil plainly infinuates : for when Boreas and his brethren were let loofe, he fays at firft *terras turbine perflant:* then adds, *incubuere mari:* to raife a tempeft on the fea was ufurpation on the prerogative of Neptune ; who had given him no leave, and therefore was enraged at his attempt.   I may alfo add, that they who are in a paffion, as Neptune then was, are apt to affume to themfelves more than is properly their due.

Line 450,   *O virgin* —— &c.

If as you feem the fifter of the day,
Or one at leaft of chafte Diana's train.

Thus, in the original.

O quam te memorem virgo——
Aut Phœbi foror, aut nympharem fanguinis una.

This is a family compliment, which Æneas here beftows on Venus. His father Anchifes had ufed the very fame to that goddefs when he courted her. This appears by that very ancient Greek poem, in

M 3

which that amour is so beautifully described, and which is thought Homer's : though it seems to be written before his age.

Line 980.   *Her princely guest was next her side.*

This I confess, is properly translated ; and according to the modern fashion of sitting at table. But the ancient custom of lying on beds, had not been understood by the unlearned reader

Æneid 2.   The destruction of Veii is here shadowed under that of Troy : Livy, in his description of it, seems to have emulated in his prose, and almost equalled the beauty of Virgil's verse.

Æneid 3.   Verse 132.

And childrens children shall the crown sustain.

Et nati natorum, & qui nascentur ab illis.

Virgil translated this verse from Homer : Homer had it from Orpheus ; and Orpheus from an ancient oracle of Apollo.   On this account it is, that Virgil immediately subjoins these words, *Hæc Phœbus, &c.*   Eustathius takes notice, that the old poets were wont to take whole paragraphs from one another, which justifies our poet for what he borrows from Homer.   Bochartus, in his letter to Segrais, mentions an oracle which he found in the fragments of an old Greek historian : the sense whereof is this in English ; that when the empire of the Priamidæ should be destroyed, the line of Anchises should succeed.   Venus therefore, says the historian, was desirous to have a son by Anchises, though he was then in his decrepid *age :* accordingly she had Æneas.   After this fhe fought occafion to ruin the race of Priam ; and fet on foot the intrigue of Alexander, (or Paris) with Helena : fhe being ravifhed, Venus pretended ftill to favour the Trojans ; left they fhould reftóre Helen, in cafe they fhould be reduced to the laft neceffity.   Whence it appears, that the controverfy betwixt Juno and Venus, was on no trivial account, but concerned the fucceffion to a great empire.

Æneid 4.   Line 945.

And muft I die, fhe faid,
And unreveng'd? 'tis doubly to be dead!
Yet even this death with pleafure I receive :
On any terms, 'tis better than to live

This is certainly the fenfe of Virgil ; on which I have paraphrafed, to make it plain.   His words are thefe ;

Moriemur inultæ ?
Sed moriamur, ait ; fic, fic juvat ire fub umbras.

Servius makes an interrogation at the word *fic* ; thus, *fic? Sic juvat ire fub umbras.* Which Mr. Cowley juftly cenfures : but his own judgment may perhaps be queftioned : for he would retrench the latter part of the verfe, and leave it an Hemiftic. *Sed moriamur, ait.* That Virgil never intended to have left any Hemiftic, I have proved already in the Preface.   That this verfe was filled up by him, with thefe words, *fic, fic juvat ire fub umbras,* is very probable ; if we confider the weight of them.   For

M 4

this procedure of Dido, does not only contain that *dira execratio quæ nullo expiatur carmine* (as Horace observes in his Canidia) but besides that, Virgil, who is full of allusions to history, under another name, describes the Decii, devoting themselves to Death this way, though in a better cause, in order to the destruction of the enemy. The reader, who will take the pains to consult Livy, in his accurate description of those Decii, thus devoting themselves, will find a great resemblance betwixt these two passages. And it is judiciously observed upon that verse,

—— *Nulla fides populis nec fœdera sunto,*

that Virgil uses the word *sunto a verbum juris,* a form of speaking on solemn and religious occasions : Livy does the like. Note also, that Dido puts herself into the Habitus Gabinus, which was the girding herself round with one sleeve of her vest, which is also according to the Roman Pontifical, in this dreadful ceremony, as Livy has observed : which is a farther confirmation of this conjecture. So that upon the whole matter, Dido only doubts whether she should die before she had taken her revenge, which she rather wished : but considering that this devoting herself was the most certain and infallible way of compassing vengeance, she thus exclaims :

Sic, sic juvat ire sub umbras :
Hauriat hunc oculis ignem crudelis ab alto
Dardanus, & nostræ secum ferat omnia mortis.

Thofe flames from far, may the falfe Trojan view;
Thofe boding omens his bafe flight purfue.

Which tranflation I take to be according to the
fenfe of Virgil. I fhould have added a note on that
former verfe,

Infelix Dido, nunc te fata impia tangunt.

Which in the édition of Heinfius is thus printed;
Nunc te faƈta impia tangunt? The word *faƈta* inftead of *fata*, is reafonably altered. For Virgil fays
afterwards, fhe died not by fate, nor by any deferved
death. *Nec fato, meritâ nec morte peribat,* &c. When
I tranflated that pafſage, I doubted of the fenfe:
and therefore omitted that Hemiftic; *Nunc te fata
impia tangunt.* But Heinfius is miftaken only in
making an interrogation point inftead of a period.
The words *faƈta impia*, I fuppofe are genuine. For fhe
had perjured herfelf in her fecond marriage; having
firmly refolved, as fhe told her fifter, in the beginning of this Æneid, never to love again, after the
death of her firft hufband; and had confirmed this
refolution by a curfe on herfelf, if fhe fhould alter it.

Sed mihi vel tellus optem, priùs ima debifcat, &c.
Ante, pudor, quàm te violem, aut tua jura refolvam.
Ille meos, primus qui me fibi junxit, amores
Abftulit: ille habeat fecum, fervetque fepulchro.

Æneid 5. A great part of this book is borrowed
from Apollonius Rhodius. And the reader may
obferve the great judgment and diftinƈtion of our
author in what he borrows from the ancients, by
comparing them. I conceive the reafon why he

omits the horfe-race in the funeral games, was becaufe he fhews Afcanius afterwards on horfeback,
with his troops of boys, and would not wear that
fubject thread-bare; which Statius, in the next age,
defcribed fo happily.   Virgil feems to me, to have
excelled Homer in all thofe fports, and to have laboured them the more in honour of Octavius, his
patron ; who inftituted the like games for perpetu-
ating the memory of his uncle Julius.   Piety, as
Virgil calls it, or dutifulnefs to parents, being a moft
popular virtue among the Romans.

Æneid 6.   Line 586.

The next in place and punifhment are they,
Who prodigally throw their lives away, &c.

Proxima forte tenent mæfti loca, qui fibi letum
Infontes peperere manu, lucemque perofi.
Projecere animas, &c.

This was taken, amongft many other things, from
the tenth book of *Plato de Republicâ :* no commen-
tator, befides Fabrini, has taken notice of it.   Self-
murder was accounted a great crime by that divine
philofopher : but the inftances which he brings, are
too many to be inferted in thefe fhort notes.   Sir
Robert Howard in his tranflation of this Æneid,
which was printed with his poems in the year 1660,
has given us the moft learned, and the moft judicious
obfervations on this book, which are extant in our
language.

Line 733.   *Lo to the secret shadows I retire,*
            To pay my penance 'till my years expire.

These two verses in English seem very different from the Latin.

Discedam; explebo numerum, reddarque tenebris.

Yet they are the sense of Virgil; at least, according to the common interpretation of this place; I will withdraw from your company; retire to the shades, and perform my penance of a thousand years; but I must confess the interpretation of those two words *explebo numerum,* is somewhat violent, if it be thus understood, *minuam numerum,* that is, I will lessen your company by my departure. For Deiphobus, being a ghost, can hardly be said to be of their number. Perhaps the poet means by *explebo numerum, absolvam sententiam* : as if Deiphobus replied to the Sibyl, who was angry at his long visit, I will only take my last leave of Æneas, my kinsman and my friend, with one hearty good wish for his health and welfare, and then leave you to prosecute your voyage. That wish is expressed in the words immediately following, *I decus, I nostrum,* &c. which contains a direct answer to what the Siybl said before, when she upbraided their long discourse, *Nos flendo ducimus horas.* This conjecture is new, and therefore left to the discretion of the reader.

Line 980.

Know first, that heav'n, and earth's compacted frame,
And flowing waters, and the starry flame,
And both the radiant lights, &c.

M 6

Principio cœlum, & terras, campofque liquentes,
Lucentemque globum lunæ titaniaque aftra, &c.

Here the fun is not expreffed, but the moon only; though a lefs, and alfo a lefs radiant light. Perhaps the copies of Virgil are all falfe; and that inftead of *titaniaque aftra*, he writ *titaniaque & aftra*; and according to thefe words I have made my tranflation. It is moft certain, that the fun ought not to be omitted, for he is frequently called the life and foul of the world. And nothing bids fo fair for a vifible divinity to thofe who know no better, than that glorious luminary. The Platonifts call God the archetypal fun, and the fun the vifible deity, the inward vital fpirit in the center of the univerfe, or that body to which that fpirit is united, and by which it exerts itfelf moft powerfully. Now it was the received hypothefis amongft the Pythagoreans, that the fun was fituate in the center of the world; Plato had it from them, and was himfelf of the fame opinion; as appears by a paffage in the Timæus: from which noble dialogue is this part of Virgil's poem taken.

Line 1156.

Great Cato there, for gravity renown'd, &c.
Quis te, magne Cato, &c.

There is no queftion but Virgil here means Cato Major, or the Cenfor. But the name of Cato being alfo mentioned in the eighth Æneid, I doubt whether he means the fame man in both places. I have faid in the Preface, that our poet was of republican

J. Collyer sculp.

principles ; and have given this for one reafon of my
opinion, that he praifed Cato in that line,

Secretifque piis, his dantem jura Catonem.

And accordingly placed him in the Elyfian fields.
Montaigne thinks this was Cato the Utican, the great
enemy of arbitrary power, and a profeffed foe to
Julius Cæfar. Ruæus would perfuade us that Virgil
meant the Cenfor. But why fhould the poet name
Cato twice, if he intended the fame perfon ? our author is too frugal of his words and fenfe, to commit
tautologies in either. His memory was not likely to
betray him into fuch an error. Neverthelefs I con-
tinue in the fame opinion concerning the principles
of our poet. He declares them fufficiently in this
book : where he praifes the firft Brutus for expelling
the Tarquins, giving liberty to Rome, and putting
to death his own children, who confpired to reftore
tyranny : he calls him only an unhappy man, for
being forced to that fevere action.

Infelix, utcunque ferent ea facta minores.
Vincet amor patriæ laudumque immenfa cupido.

Let the reader weigh thefe two verfes, and he
muft be convinced that I am in the right : and that
I have not much injured my mafter in my tranflation of them.

Line 1143.

Embrace again, my fons ; be foes no more ;
Nor ftain your country with her childrens gore.
And thou the firft lay down thy lawlefs claim ;
Thou of my blood, who bear'ft the Jullan name.

This note, which is out of its proper place, I deferred on purpose, to place it here: becaufe it difcovers the principles of our poet more plainly than any of the reft.

Tuque prior, tu parce, genus qui ducis Olympo,
Projice tela manu, fanguis meus!

Anchifes here fpeaks to Julius Cæfar; and commands him firft to lay down his arms, which is a plain condemnation of his caufe. Yet obferve our poet's incomparable addrefs: for though he fhews himfelf fufficiently to be a commonwealth's-man; yet in refpect to Auguftus, who was his patron, he ufes the authority of a parent, in the perfon of Anchifes; who had more right lay this injunction on Cæfar than on Pompey; becaufe the latter was not of his blood. Thus our author cautioufly veils his own opinion, and takes fanctuary under Anchifes; as if that ghoft would have laid the fame command on Pompey alfo, had he been lineally defcended from him.. What could be more judicioufly contrived, when this was the Æneid which he chofe to read before his mafter?

Line 1221.

A new Marcellus fhall arife in thee.

In Virgil thus:
Tu Marcellus eris.

How unpoetically and baldly had this been tranflated; *Thou fhalt Marcellus be!* Yet fome of my friends were of opinion, that I miftook the fenfe of Virgil in my tranflation. The French interprete:

obferves nothing on this place ; but that it appears
by it, the mourning of Octavia was yet frefh, for the
lofs of her fon Marcellus, whom fhe had by her firft
hufband : and who died in the year *ab urbe conditâ*,
731, and collects from thence that Virgil, reading
this Æneid before her, in the fame year, had juft
finifhed it : that from this time to that of the poet's
death, was little more than four years. So that fup-
pofing him to have written the whole Æneis in
eleven years ; the firft fix books muft have taken up
feven of thofe years : on which account, the fix laft
muft of neceffity be lefs correct.

Now for the falfe judgment of my friends, there
is but this little to be faid for them ; the words of
Virgil in the verfe preceding are thefe,

—— *Siqua fata afpera rumpas.*

As if the poet had meant, If you break through your
hard deftiny, fo as to be born, you fhall be called
Marcellus : but this cannot be the fenfe : for though
Marcellus was born, yet he broke not through thofe
hard decrees, which doomed him to fo immature a
death.   Much lefs can Virgil mean, you fhall be the
fame Marcellus by the tranfmigration of his foul.
For according to the fyftem of our author, a thoufand years muft be firft elapfed, before the foul can
return into a human body ; but the firft Marcellus
was flain in the fecond Punick war.   And how
many hundred years were yet wanting, to the ac-
complifhing his penance, may with eafe be gathered,
by computing the time betwixt Scipio and Auguftus.
By which it is plain, that Virgil cannot mean the

same Marcellus; but one of his defcendants; whom
I call a new Marcellus; who fo much refembled his
anceftor, perhaps in his features, and his perfon,
but certainly in his military virtues, that Virgil cries
out, *quantum inftar in ipfo eft!* which I have tranflated,

> *How like the former, and almoft the fame.*

Line 1235.

> *Two gates the filent houfe of Sleep adorn;*
> *Of polifh'd iv'ry this; that of tranfparent horn.*

Virgil borrowed this imagination from Homer,
Odyffes the 9th, line 562. The tranflation gives
the reafon, why true prophetic dreams are faid to
pafs through the gate of horn, by adding the epithet
tranfparent: which is not in Virgil; whofe words
are only thefe;

> *Sunt geminæ Somni portæ; quarum altera fertur*
> *Cornea ——*

What is pervious to the fight is clear; and (alluding to this property,) the poet infers fuch dreams
are of divine revelation. Such as pafs through the
ivory gate, are of the contrary nature; polifhed lies.
But there is a better reafon to be given. For the
ivory alludes to the teeth, the horn to the eyes.
What we fee is more credible, than what we only
hear; that is, words that pafs through the portal of
the mouth, or hedge of the teeth: (which is Homer's expreffion for fpeaking.)

Æneid 7. Line 169.

Strange to relate, the flames involv'd in smoke, &c.

Virgil, in this place takes notice of a great secret in the Roman divination: the lambent fires, which rose above the head, or played about it, were signs of posterity; such were those which he observed in the second Æneid: which were seen mounting from the crown of Ascanius;

Ecce levis summo de vertice visus Iuli
Fundere lumen apex.

Smoky flames (or involved in smoke) were of a mixed omen; such were those which are here described: for smoke signifies tears, because it produces them, and flames happiness. And therefore Virgil says, that this ostent was not only *mirabile visu*, but *horrendum.*

Line 367.

One only daughter heirs my crown and state.

This has seemed to some an odd passage: that a king should offer his daughter and heir to a stranger prince, and a wanderer, before he had seen him, and when he had only heard of his arrival on his coasts: but these criticks have not well considered the simplicity of former times; when the heroines almost courted the marriage of illustrious men. Yet Virgil here observes the rule of decency; Lavinia offers not herself: it is Latinus who propounds the match: and he had been foretold, both by an augur, and an oracle, that he should have a foreign son in-law; who was also a hero. Fathers, in those an-

cient ages, confidering birth and virtue, more than
fortune, in the placing of their daughters. Which
I could prove by various examples ; the contrary of
which being now practifed, I dare not fay in our
nation, but in France, has not a little darkened the
luftre of their nobility. That Lavinia was averfe to
this marriage, and for what reafon, I fhall prove in
its proper place.

Line 1020.

—— *And where Abella fees,*
From her high tow'rs, the harveft of her trees.

I obferve that Virgil names not Nola, which was
not far diftant from Abella ; perhaps, becaufe that
city, (the fame in which Auguftus died afterwards,)
had once refufed to give him entertainment ; if we
may believe the author of his life. Homer heartily
curfes another city which had ufed him in the fame
manner : but our author thought his filence of the
Nolans a fufficient correction. When a poet paffes
by a place or perfon, though a fair occafion offers of
remembering them, it is a fign he is, or thinks himfelf, much difobliged.

Æneid 8. Line 34.

So when the fun by day, or moon by night,
Strike on the polifh'd brafs their trembling light, &c.

This fimilitude is literally taken from Apollonius Rhodius ; and it is hard to fay, whether the
original or the tranflation excels. But in the fhield
which he defcribes afterwards in this Æneid, he as
much tranfcends his mafter Homer as the arms.

of Glaucus were richer than thofe of Diomedes.
Χρύσεα Χαλκείων.

.Lines 115, and 116.
Æneas takes the mother and her brood,
And all on Juno's altar are beftow'd.

The tranflation is infinitely fhort of Virgil, whofe
words are thefe;

—— *Tibi* enim, *tibi maxima Juno*
Mactat facra ferens, & cum grege fiftit ad aram.

For I could not turn the word *enim* into Englifh
with any grace, though it was of fuch neceffity, in
the Roman rites, that a faerifice could not be performed without it; it is of the fame nature (if I
may prefume to name that facred myftery) in our
words of confecration at the altar.

Æneid 9.   Lines 853, 854.
At the full ftretch of both his hands, he drew;
And almoft join'd the horns of the tough eugh.

The firft of thefe lines is all of monofyllables, and
both verfes are very rough : but of choice ; for it
had been eafy for me to have fmoothed them. But
either my ear deceives me, or they exprefs the thing
which I intended in their found. For the ftrefs of a
bow which is drawn to the full exent, is expreffed
in the harfhnefs of the firft verfe, clogged not only
with monofyllables, but with confonants; and thefe
words, *the tough eugh*, which conclude the fecond
line, feem as forceful, as they are unharmonious.
Homer and Virgil are both frequent in their adapting

founds to the thing they fignify. One example wilt
ferve for both ; becaufe Virgil borrowed the following verfes from Homer's Odyffes.

Unà eurufque notufque ruunt creberque procellis
Africus, & vaftos volvunt ad litora fluctus.

Σὸν δ' Εὖροσε, Νότοσε ἴπισεν, Ζέφυροσε δυσαὴς
Καὶ Βορίης αἰθρυγενετὴς, μέγα κῦμα κυλίνδων.

Our language is not often capable of thefe beauties : though fometimes I have copied them, of
which thefe verfes are an inftance.

Line 1095.

——————— *His ample fhield*
Is falfify'd ; and round with jav'lins fill'd.

When I read this Æneid to many of my friends,
in company together, moft of them quarrelled at the
word *falfified,* as an innovation in our language.
The fact is confeffed ; for I remember not to have
read it in any Englifh author; though perhaps it
may be found in Spencer's Fairy Queen : but fuppofe it be not there : why am I forbidden to borrow
from the Italian, (a polifhed language) the word
which is wanting in my native tongue? Terence
has often Grecifed : Lucretius has followed his example : and pleaded for it ; *fic quia me cogit patrii*
fermonis Egeftas. Virgil has confirmed it by his frequent practice, and even Cicero in profe, wanting
terms of philofophy in the Latin tongue, has taken
them from Ariftotle's Greek. Horace has given us
a rule for coining words, *fi Græco fonte cadant.* Ef-

pecially, when other words are joined with them, which explain the sense. I use the word *falsify* in this place, to mean that the shield of Turnus was not of proof against the spears and javelins of the Trojans; which had pierced it through and through (as we say) in many places. The words which accompany this new one, make my meaning plain; according to the precept which Horace gave. But I said I borrowed the word from the Italian: *Vide* Ariosto, *Cant.* 26.

> *Ma si l' Usbergo d' ambi era perfetto*
> *Che mai poter falsarlo in nessum canto.*

Falsar cannot be otherwise turned, than by *falsified*; for *his shield was falsed*, is not English. I might indeed have contented myself with saying his shield was pierced, and bored, and stuck with *javelins; nec sufficit umbo ictibus.* They who will not admit a new word, may take the old, the matter is not worth dispute.

Æneid 10. Line 312.
A choir of nereids, &c.

These were transformed from ships to sea-nymphs: this is almost as violent a machine, as the death of Aruns by a goddess in the Episode of Camilla. But the poet makes use of it with greater art: for here it carries on the main design. These new made divinities, not only tell Æneas what had passed in his camp during his absence; and what was the present distress of his besieged people; and that his horsemen,

whom he had fent by land, were ready to join him
at his defcent; but warn him to provide for battle the
next day, and foretel him good fuccefs. So that
this epifodical machine is properly a part of the
great poem : for befides what I have faid, they pufh
on his navy with celeftial vigor, that it might reach
the port more fpeedily, and take the enemy more
unprovided to refift the landing.   Whereas the machine relating to Camilla, is only ornamental : for
it has no effect which I can find, but to pleafe the
reader, who is concerned, that her death fhould be
revenged.

Lines 241, 242.
Now facred fifters open all your fpring,
The Tufcan leaders, and their army, fing;

The poet here begins to tell the names of the
Tufcan captains who followed Æneas to the war :
and I obferve him to be very particular in the defcription of their perfons, and not forgetful of their
manners: exact alfo in the relation of the numbers
which each of them command.   I doubt not but
as in the fifth book, he gave us the names of the
champions, who contended for the feveral prizes,
that he might oblige many of the moft ancient Roman families, their defcendants; and as in the 7th
book, he muftered the auxiliary forces of the Latins,
on the fame account; fo here he gratifies his Tufcan friends, with the like remembrance of their anceftors; and above the reft, Mecænas his great patron;
who being of a royal family in Etruria, was probably
reprefented under one of the names here mentioned,

then known among the Romans, though at so great
a diftance unknown to us.   And for his fake
chiefly, as I guefs, he makes Æneas (by whom he
always means Auguftus) to feek for aid in the country of Mecænas, thereby to endear his protector to
his emperor ; as if there had been a former friendfhip betwixt their lines.   And who knows, but
Mecænas might pretend that the Cilnian family was
derived from Tarchon, the chief commander of the
Tufcans ?

Line 622.
Nor I his mighty fire could ward the blow.

I have mentioned this paffage in my preface to the
Æneis, to prove, that Fate was fuperior to the gods;
and that Jove could neither defer nor alter its decrees.
Sir Robert Howard has fince been pleafed to fend
me the concurrent teftimony of Ovid : it is in the
laft book of his Metamorphofes: where Venus com-
plains, that her defcendant, Julius Cæfar, was in
danger of being murdered by Brutus and Caffius, at
the head of the Commonwealth faction, and defires
them to prevent that barbarous affaffination.   They
are moved to compaffion ; they are concerned for
Cæfar ; but the poet plainly tells us, that it was not
in their power to change deftiny : all they could do,
was to teftify their forrow for his approaching death
by forefhewing it with figns and prodigies, as appears by the following lines,

Talia nequicquam toto Venus aurea Cœlo
Verba jacit : fuperofque movet : qui rumpere quanquam

Ferrea non poſſunt veterum decreta ſororum,
Signa tamen luctus dant haud incerta futuri.

Then ſhe addreſſes to her father Jupiter, hoping
aid from him becauſe he was thought omnipotent.
But he, it ſeems, could do as little as the reſt, for
he anſwers thus :

> ———— *ſola inſuperabile fatum*
> *Nata, movere paras ? intres licet ipſa ſororum*
> *Tecta trium ; cernes illic molimine vaſto*
> *Ex ære, & ſolido rerum tabularia ferro :*
> *Quæ neque concurſum cœli, neque fulminis iram,*
> *Nec metuunt ullas tuta atque æterna ruinas.*
> *Invenies illic inciſa adamante perenni*
> *Fata tui generis, legi ipſe, animoque notavi,*
> *Et referam : ne ſis etiamnum ignara futuri.*
> *Hic ſua complevit (pro quo Cytherea laboras,)*
> *Tempora, perfectis quos terræ debuit, annis,* &c.

Jupiter you ſee is only library-keeper, or *cuſtos
rotulorum* to the Fates : for he offers his daughter a
caſt of his office, to give her a ſight of their decrees ;
which the inferior gods were not permitted to read
without his leave.   This agrees with what I have
ſaid already in the preface ; that they not having ſeen
the records, might believe they were his own hand-
writing ; and conſequently at his diſpoſing either to
blot out, or alter, as he ſaw convenient.   And of
this opinion was Juno in theſe words, *tua qui potes
orſa reflectas.*   Now the abode of thoſe deſtinies being in Hell, we cannot wonder why the ſwearing by
Styx was an inviolable oath amongſt the gods of

heaven, and that Jupiter himfelf fhould fear to be
accufed of forgery by the Fates, if he altered any
thing in their decrees. Chaos, Night, and Erebus,
being the moft ancient of the deities, and inftituting
thofe fundamental laws, by which he was afterwards
to govern. Hefiod gives us the genealogy of the
gods, and I think I may fafely infer the reft. I will
only add, that Homer was more a fatalift than Virgil:
for it has been obferved, that the word τυχη, or
fortune, is not to be found in his two poems; but
inftead of it, always μοιρα.

Æneid 12. Line 808, and 809.

Sea-born Meffapus, with Atinas, heads
The Latin fquadrons; and to battle leads.

The poet had faid, in the preceding lines, that
Mneftheus, Serefthus, and Afylas, led on the Trojans, the Tufcans, and the Arcadians: but none of
the printed copies, which I have feen, mention any
leader of the Rutulians and Latins, but Meffapus the
fon of Neptune. Ruæus takes notice of this paffage,
and feems to wonder at it; but gives no reafon,
why Meffapus is alone without a coadjutor.

The four verfes of Virgil run thus.

Totæ adeò converfæ acies, omnefque Latini,
Omnes Dardanidæ; Mneftheus, acerque Serefthus,
Et Meffapus equum domitor, & fortis Afylas,
Tufcorumque Phalanx, Evandrique Arcadis alæ.

I doubt not but the third line was originally thus,

Et Meffapus equûm domitor, & fortis Atinas:

For the two names of Aſylas and Atinas are ſo like, that one might eaſily be miſtaken for the other by the tranſcribers. And to fortify this opinion, we find afterward, in the relation of Sages to Turnus, that Atinas is joined with Meſſapus.

Soli, pro portis, Meſſapus & acer Atinas
Saſtentant aciem ———

In general I obſerve, not only in this Æneid, but in all the ſix laſt books, that Æneas is never ſeen on horſeback, and but once before as I remember, in the fourth, when he hunts with Dido. The reaſon of this, if I gueſs aright, was a ſecret compliment which the poet made to his countrymen the Romans ; the ſtrength of whoſe armies conſiſted moſt in foot ; which, I think, were all Romans and Italians. But their wings or ſquadrons were made up of their *allies,* who were foreigners.

Æneid 12.   Lines 100, 101, 102.

At this a flood of tears Lavinia ſhed ;
A crimſon bluſh her beauteous face o'erſpread,   }
Varying her cheeks, by turns, with white and red.

Amata, ever partial to the cauſe of Turnus, had juſt before deſired him, with all manner of earneſt-neſs, not to engage his rival in ſingle fight ; which was his preſent reſolution. Virgil, though in favour of his hero, he never tells us directly, that Lavinia preferred Turnus to Æneas, yet has inſinuated this preference twice before. For mark, in the 7th Æneid, ſhe left her father, who had promiſed her to Æneas without afking her confent : and followed her mother into the woods, with a troop of Bacchanals, where Amata fung the marriage fong, in the name of Turnus ; which if fhe had difliked, fhe might have oppofed.   Then in the 11th Æneid, when her mother went to the temple of Pallas, to invoke her aid againft Æneas, whom fhe calls by no better name than Phrygius Prædo, Lavinia fits by her in the fame chair or litter, *juxtaque comes Lavinia virgo,* ———— *Oculos dejeƐta decoros.*   What greater fign of love, than fear and concernment for the lover ? In the lines which I have quoted fhe not only fheds tears, but changes colour.   She had been bred up with Turnus, and Æneas was wholly a ftranger to her.   Turnus in all probability was her firft love ;. and favoured by her mother, who had the afcendant over her father.   But I am much deceived, if (befides what I have faid) there be not a fecret fatire againft the fex, which is lurking under this defcription of Virgil, who feldom fpeaks well of women : better indeed of Camilla, than any other ; for he commends her beauty and valour, becaufe he would concern the reader for her death.   But valour is no very proper praife for womankind ; and beauty is common to the fex.   He fays alfo fomewhat of Andromache, but tranfiently : and his Venus is a better mother than a wife, for fhe owns to Vulcan fhe had a fon by another man.   The reft are Juno's, Diana's Dido's, Amata's, two mad prophetefles, three harpies on earth, and as many furies under ground. This fable of Lavinia includes a fecret moral ;. that

women in their choice of husbands, prefer the
younger of their suitors to the elder ; are insensible
of merit, fond of handsomness ; and, generally
speaking, rather hurried away by their appetite, than
governed by their reason.

Line 1191, and 1192.

This let me beg, (and this no fates, withstand)
Both for myself, and for your father's land, &c.

The words in the original are these, *pro latio ob-*
testor, pro majestate tuorum. Virgil very artfully uses
here the word *majestas,* which the Romans loved so
well, that they appropriated it to themselves. *Ma-*
jestas populi Romani. This title applied to kings, is
very modern, and that is all I will say of it at present : though the word requires a larger note. In
the word *tuorum,* is included the sense of my transla-
tion, *Your father's land :* because Saturn, the father
of Jove, had governed that part of Italy, after his
expulsion from Crete. But that on which I most
insist, is the address of the poet, in this speech of
Juno. Virgil was sufficiently sensible, as I have said
in the preface, that whatever the common opinion
was, concerning the descent of the Romans from the
Trojans ; yet the ancient customs, rites, laws, and
habits of those Trojans were wholly lost, and perhaps also that they had never been : and for this
reason, he introduces Juno in this place, requesting
of Jupiter, that no memory might remain of Troy
(the town she hated) that the people hereafter should
not be called Trojans, nor retain any thing which be-

longed to their predeceffors. And why might not this alfo be concerted betwixt our author and his friend Horace, to hinder Auguftus from rebuilding Troy, and removing thither the feat of empire, a defign fo unpleafing to the Romans? but of this I am not pofitive, becaufe I have not confulted d'Acier, and the reft of the criticks, to afcertain the time in which Horace writ the Ode relating to that fubject.

Line 1224, and 1225.

Deep in the difmal regions, void of light,
Three fifters at a birth, were born to Night.

The father of thefe, (not here mentioned) was Acheron: the names of the three, were Alecto, Megæra, and Tifiphone.   They were called Furies in hell, on earth Harpies, and in heaven Diræ: two of thefe affifted at the throne of Jupiter, and were employed by him, to punifh the wickednefs of mankind. Thefe two muft be Megæra, and Tifiphone: not Alecto, for Juno exprefsly commands her to return to hell, from whence fhe came; and gives this reafon:

Te fuper Ætherias errare licentiùs auras,
Haud pater ipfe velit fummi regnator Olympi:
Cede locis.

Probably this Dira, un-named by the poet in this place, might be Tifiphone; for though we find her in hell, in the fixth Æneid, employed in the punifhment of the damned,

Continuo fontes ultrix accincta flagello
Tifiphone quatit infultans, &c.

Yet afterwards fhe is on earth in the tenth Æneid, and amidft the battle, *Pallida Tifiphone media inter millia fævit.* Which I guefs to be Tifiphone, the rather, by the etymology of her name; which is compounded of Τίω *ulcifcor*; and φόνο· *cædes.* Part of her errand being to affright Turnus with the flings of a guilty confcience; and denounce vengeance againft him for breaking the firft treaty, by refufing to yield Lavinia to Æneas, to whom fhe was promifed by her father, and confequently, for being the author of an unjuft war; and alfo for violating the fecond treaty, by declining the fingle combat, which he had ftipulated with his rival, and called the gods to witnefs before their altars. As for the names of the harpies, (fo called on earth) Hefiod tells us they were Iris, Aello, and Ocypete. Virgil calls one of them Celæno: this I doubt not was Alecto; whom Virgil calls in the third Æneid, *Furiarum maxima:* and in the fixth again, by the fame name —— *Furiarum maxima, juxta accubat.* That fhe was the chief of the furies, appears by her defcription in the feventh Æneid: to which, for hafte, I refer the reader.

F I N I S.

INDEX

PASTORALS.

BY MR. POTTER.

N. B. *The Subject of each* PASTORAL *may be seen by the* ARGUMENT.

PERSONS AND THINGS.

A.

	Paſt.	Ver.
ACHILLES — — —	iv	44
Adonis — — —	x	26
Ægle — — — —	vi	32
Ægon — — — —	iii	2
—— the owner of ſheep kept by Damætas	iii	2
—— courted Neæra, but ſlighted by her	iii	4
—— (Lictian) to join in the annual ſong to the memory of Daphnis —	v	114
Ænigma, one propoſed by Damætas —	iii	160
——————, one propoſed by Menalcas —	iii	163

VOL. IV.   O

INDEX of Persons and Things.

B.

C.

Q. 2.

Paſt. Ver.

O 3

INDEX of PERSONS and THINGS.

INDEX of Persons and Things.

INDEX of Persons and Things:

INDEX

TO THE

GEORGICS.

By Mr. POTTER.

N. B. *The Subject of each* GEORGIC *may be seen by the* ARGUMENT.

PERSONS AND THINGS.

A.

P 2

L.

V.

W.

GENERAL

GENERAL INDEX

TO THE

GEORGICS.

The GEORGICS comprehend a Syftem of the moft material branches of AGRICULTURE, and RURAL ARTS; under four diftinct heads: *viz.* TILLAGE; PLANTING; KNOWLEDGE of ANIMALS; and the NATURE and MANAGEMENT of BEES.

N. B. *The figures mark the verfe of each Book.*

GEORGIC I. Of TILLAGE, &c.

Lands] BARREN, require early tillage, 96; fhould not be ploughed deep, 101; fhould be burnt, 123.—Watry lands fhould be tilled but feldom, 108.—Lands, where tares and vetches have grown, will produce plentiful crops of corn the fucceeding year, 112.—Lands for grain fhould be drained from water, 169.—The proper time for draining lands, is the fpring and autumn, 171.

GENERAL INDEX

Soil] Thofe that are meagre by nature may be improved by the change of feed, 120.

Ground] Fallow, requires fprinkling with afhes, and fatening dung, 119.

Earth] The clods fhould be fmoothed with harrows, or broke with rakes, after grain is fown, 138.

Ploughing] The Spring a proper time for it, 69; alfo in Autumn, 3eo. Ploughing acrofs the furrows profitable, 141.

Sowing] The feafon for it;—of wheat, 310;—other forts of feeds, 316.

Grain] Of all kinds fhould be occafionally changed to avoid degeneration, 286.

Seeds] How to fow particular forts, 302. Should be covered as foon as fown, 152.

Corn] When grown to the height of the furrows, fhould be cropped by fheep, to prevent a weaknefs of ftalk, 165.

Seafons] Summer, the proper employments of it, for the hufbandn h, 397.—Winter, the employments fuitable to it, 350;—the time to thrafh the wood for maft of oak, 409;—other employments fuitable to it, 411. —A dry winter favourable to fown feeds, 145.

GEORGIC II. PLANTING, &c.

Trees] What owe their birth from nature, 13. Raifed from feeds, 19. Some require no root, 37. What may be grafted, 43. Thofe that advance to great heights are barren, 67. Barren ones capable of being grafted to bear, 71. Many that are barren by growing wild, improve and bear by being tranfplanted, 76. Such as fpring from feeds, are flow of growth, 81. Their wildnefs may be tamed by art and labour, 85. What may be raifed from cyons, 93. What forts will receive grafts, 96. Trees know their refpective countries, 162. What trees are peculiar to particular countries, 163. Hazle-trees are injurious to vineyards, 410. Apple-trees require no props till over-

GEORGIC III. Of Animals, &c.

GEORGIC IV. Of BEES, &c.

INDEX

I N D E X

TO THE

Æ N E I S.

BY MR. POTTER.

N. B. *The general Subject of each Book may be seen
by the* ARGUMENT.

PERSONS AND THINGS.

A.

	Book.	Ver.
ABBAS — — — —	i	173
Abella — — — —	vii	1020
Aceſtes — — — — —	i	171
—— receives Æneas hoſpitably —	v	48
—— reproaches Entellus for not entering into combat with Dares —	v	513
—— enters the liſt of Archers —	v	662
—— his arrow fired into flames by its ſwiftneſs	v	691
—— is preſented with the prize by Æneas	v	704
Achates, urges Æneas to diſcover himſelf to Dido	i	815

INDEX of Persons and Things.

R 2

INDEX of PERSONS and THINGS.

INDEX of PERSONS and THINGS.

J.

S 3

INDEX of Persons and Things.

N.

P.

INDEX of Persons and Things.

T.

V.

INDEX of PERSONS and THINGS:

A

POETICAL INDEX

TO

VIRGIL's ÆNEIS.

BY MR. POTTER.

N. B. *The first Number marks the Book, the second the Verse.*

FABLE.

THE great *Moral of the Æneis*, is *pious resignation and its rewards*; which is pursued through the whole fable.

EPISODES or FABLES *interwoven into the Poem, but foreign to its design.*

The history of the fate of Troy, and the adventures of Æneas after the siege, as related by him to Dido, Book the second and third, may be considered as such. The friendship of Nisus and Euryalus, ix. 222, &c. &c. The different actions and death of Lausus and Mezentius, x. The Episode of Camilla, xi. 815.

U 2

F A B L E.

Allegorical FABLES.

Moral.] Punishment of a voluptuary after death, vi. 8 *to.*
And all the descriptions of punishments for particular
crimes in B. vi.

Physical or Philosophical.] See the system of Platonick
philosophy, relative to the soul of man, in the ALLE-
GORIES.

For the rest of the Allegories, *see the* System of the
Gods *as acting in their allegorical characters, under the
article* CHARACTERS.

Allegorical or Fictitious Persons in VIRGIL.

Æolus the god of the winds, i. 79. The sea-nymphs,
i. 205. Triton, i. 205. x. 298. Celæno, one of
the harpies, iii. 322. Scylla, (the rock) personified,
iii. 540. Fame, iv. 252. xi. 209. xii. 883. Atlas,
iv. 364. Iris, or the Rainbow, iv. 996. The messenger of Juno, v. 791. ix. 2. Alecto, one of the
Furies, vii. 451. The choir of Nereids, x. 312.
Juturna, x. 618. The Dira, or Fury, xii. 1239.

The MARVELLOUS *or supernatural* FICTIONS *in* VIRGIL.

The sea-nymphs assisting the Trojans to get their ships
off the rocks, after the storm, i. 205. The cloud
concealing Æneas when he entered Carthage, i. 613.
Cupid personating Ascanius, i. 965. The prodigy of
the serpents destroying Laocoön and his children, at
Troy, as related by Æneas, ii. 269. Omen of the
lambent fire round the crown of Iülus (or Ascanius)
ii. 930. Creüsa's Ghost appearing to Æneas, as related by him, ii. 1047. Prodigy of the Myrtles
weeping blood, iii. 36. The Ghost of Polydore ad-

FABLE.

dressing Æneas, iii. 58. The prediction of the Oracle,. iii. 127. The interpretation of the Oracle by the household Gods of Æneas, iii. 208. The prophecy of the Harpy, iii. 333. The portents observed by Dido on the departure of Æneas from Carthage, iv. 657. Iris cutting Dido's fatal lock, iv. 1009. Her descent to the Trojan matrons, v 787. Also to Turnus, ix. 2. Prodigy of the serpent from the Tomb of Anchises,. v. 111. Of an arrow firing with the violence of its way, v. 691. The miraculous shower, sent by Jupiter to extinguish the flames of the Trojan fleet, v. 910. The Ghost of Anchises, v. 945, and all the spirits of departed persons, in the shades below, vi. 455, throughout. The descent of Sleep, v. 1090. The golden branch of Proserpine's tree, vi. 210. The doves directing Æneas to the tree, vi. 288. The marvellous river Styx, vi. 503. ix. 120. Cerberus watching the gate of Hell, vi. 564. Elysium, vi. 868. The prodigy of Lavinia's hair firing at the altar, vii. 111. The interpositions of Alecto, vii. 479, &c. Juno's unbaring the gates of the temple of Mars, vii. 857. Tiber (the God of the River) appearing to Æneas while asleep, viii. 46. The prodigy of the fatal swine, and thirty young ones, viii. 111, of Æneas being called to the war, by the sound of warlike instruments, and appearance of arms in the sky, by the device of Venus, viii. 692. The changing of the Trojan ships to sea-nymphs, ix. 139. Jupiter bowing the heavens, at the request of Ascanius, ix. 863. Apollo bestriding a golden cloud, and animating Ascanius to glory, ix 873. Juno's directing the lance thrown by Pandarus, from Turnus, ix. 1007. Jove's sending Iris to force Turnus from the Trojans, ix. 1086. The choir of sea-nymphs surrounding Æneas's ship, x 324. Venus directing the arrows of the Enemy from Æneas, x. 457. Juturna's interpositions, x. 618. xii 340 —689.—1035. The device of Juno to convey Turnus from the war, x. 896. The

FABLE.

death of Aruns, by the Goddefs Opis, xi. 1246. The interpofition of Jupiter in behalf of the Trojans, xi. 1069. The prodigy of jove's bird, xii. 370. Of Venus healing the wound of Æneas, xii. 609. Jupiter weighing the fate of Æneas and Turnus in his balance, xii. 1054. Prodigy of Æneas's lance ftuck in the olive-tree, xii. 1119. Venus freeing the lance, xii. 1138. The Dira, or Fury, fent by Jupiter to drive Juturna from the war, xii. 1237. Prodigy of a great ftone heaved by Turnus, of weight equal to the ftrength of twelve men, xii. 1300. The Fury rendering all the attempts of Turnus vain, xii. 1321.

Under this head, may alfo be included the paffions in human and vifible forms, and the reft.

CHARACTERS or MANNERS.

Charaders of the Gods of VIRGIL, as acting in the Phyfical or Moral capacities of thofe Deities.

JUPITER.

Acting and governing all, as the fupreme Being.] Interpofes in favour of the Trojans, from B. ix. to the end of the Poem. *See the Article* THEOLOGY *in the next Index.*

JUNO.

As Goddefs of Empire.] Prefides over marriage rites, iv. 80. xii. 1194. An Enemy to Æneas and the Trojans, through the whole Poem. Endeavours to pre-

POETICAL INDEX.

CHARACTERS.

vent the Trojans from settling in Italy, i. 106.
*See the Table of marvellous and supernatural Fictions,
for the instances of her interpositions against the Trojans,
and in favour of Turnus.*

APOLLO.

As the Sun.] Restores the day, i. 422. Scorches the
sky, vii. 997.
As Destiny.] Taught Helenus the gift of Prophesy, iii.
461. Inspires prophesy, iii. 552. Directed the fate
of Æneas, iii 616. Acquaints Ascanius of his future fortune, ix. 876.

MARS.

As God of War.] Inspires the Latians with courage,
and chills the hearts of the Trojans, ix. 973.

VENUS.

As the passion of Love.] Makes Cupid personate Ascanius, to inflame Dido with a passion for Æneas, i.
946. Inspires Vulcan to forge arms for Æneas, viii.
514.
As the parent of Æneas.] Attends the fortune of the
Trojans, and favours them through the whole Poem.

CUPID.

As God of Love.] Inflames Dido with a passion for
Æneas, i. 1005.

POETICAL INDEX.

CHARACTERS.

NEPTUNE.

As God of the Sea.] Superior to all other watry deities, i. 176, 191. Calms the Storm raised by Æolus, i. 203. Favours the Trojans, i. 208.

VULCAN.

Or the Element of Fire.] Reigns triumphant at the firing of the Trojan fleet, v. 863. Directs the Cyclops to forge the fated arms for Æneas, viii. 578.

MERCURY.

As Messenger of Jupiter.] Is sent to gain the Trojans a favourable reception at Carthage, i. 408. Warns Æneas from Carthage, iv. 350, 805.

CHARACTERS of the HEROES.

N. B. *The Speeches which depend upon, and flow from, these several characters, are distinguished by an S.*

ÆNEAS.

Pious to the Gods, i. 277. S. v. 70. S. 910. S. viii. 719. xi. 5, 488. xii. 266. S.
Filial and parental, ii. 982, 1094. xii. 642.
A lover of his people, i. 424, 644, S. ii. 3.
Tender and compassionate, v. 1433. vi. 257. x. 1165, xi. 43 57. xii. 1362.
Eloquent in all his Orations and Speeches.
Superior to all men in valour, throughout.

POETICAL INDEX.

CHARACTERS.

TURNUS.

Ambitious, fiery, and undaunted, vii. 795. ix. 53, 153.
Revengeful and implacable, as well as valiant, throughout.

ASCANIUS.

Sensible, v. 876. S.
Manly, vii. 687. ix. 417.
Filial, xii. 568.
Valiant, v. 745. ix. 806, 868.

PALLAS.

Friendly, viii. 161. S.
Valiant, x. 510, 630. S.

TARCHON.

Valiant, xi. 1073, 1118.

MEZENTIUS.

Valiant, and undaunted, x. 977, 1257.
Parental, x. 1206.
Haughty, cruel, irreligious, a blasphemer, vii. 895.
viii. 10. x. 1026, 1046, 1096.

LAUSUS.

Skilful, and heroic, vii. 899. x. 601.
Eminently filial and pious, x. 1121, 1131.

MESSAPUS.

Brave, and a Warrior, vii. 955. viii. 9, 693.

POETICAL INDEX.

CHARACTERS.

DRANCES.

Envious, factious, cautious in battle, a caballer, and tongue-valiant, xi. 183, 510, &c.

CHARACTERS of other HEROES.

Acestes, friendly and benevolent, v. 48, 80. A skilful archer, v. 685.

Accestes, faithful, xi. 45, 123.

Achates, faithful to Æneas, and the Trojan interest, i. 173, 815, 911. viii. 610, and throughout the Poem.

Acmon, brave, x. 188.

Alethes, pious, affectionate and sensible, ix. 326.

Asius, heroic, x. 188.

Asylas, skilful in throwing the javelin, ix. 777. A skilful soothsayer and augur, x. 255.

Bitias, presuming, and rashly valiant, ix. 918.

Clausus, an experienced general, vii. 973.

Entellus, valiant, v. 606, 633.

Evander, friendly, benevolent, sensible, pious and parental, viii 205, 269, 679, 731, 754.

Euryalus, beautiful, eminently heroic, inconsiderate, but singular in friendship, ix. 414, 460.

Haleius, heroic, proud, fierce and rash, vii. 1000. x. 577, &c.

Hæmon, resolute, ix. 932. x. 189.

Hæmonides, (priest of Apollo) proud and cowardly, x. 747, &c.

Helenus, (a prophet and hero) friendly, learned, eloquent, pious, and generously benevolent, iii. 446, 480, 592.

CHARACTERS.

Ilioneus, sensible and eloquent; see his speeches, i. 734.
vii. 291. Compassionate, ix. 664.

Latinus, friendly, hospitable, deliberate, penetrating,
pious, and resigned to fate, vii. 268, 354, 813. xi.
355. 463. xii. 31.

Lucagus, bold, x. 810.

Nisus, famous for swiftness, sensible, prudent, and valiant, v. 418. ix. 440. His singular friendship and
tenderness for Euryalus, v. 437. ix. 266, 531, 571,
953.

Pandarus, presuming, and rashly valiant, ix. 914.

Sergesthus, faithful and brave, ix. 216.

Ufens, a bold warrior, viii. 9.

SPEECHES and ORATIONS.

A TABLE of the most important in the ÆNEIS.

In the Exhortatory or Deliberative kind.

The complaint of Venus to Jupiter, i. 314. Of Venus
to Æneas, i 536. Of Venus to Cupid, i. 937. Of
Celæno to the Trojans, iii. 324. Of Juno to Venus,
iv. 161. Of Mercury to Æneas, iv. 389, 806. Of
Dido on the departure of Æneas, iv. 848. Of Nautes
to Æneas, v. 928. Of the Sibyl to Æneas, vi. 191.
To Charon, vi 538. Juno's Speech, on the Trojans
landing at Laurentum, vii. 404. Of Juno to Alecto,

SPEECHES.

vii 469, 765. Of Turnus to his troops, ix. 155. Of Nisus to Euryalus, ix. 235. Of Jupiter to the gods in council, x. 7, 159. Of Pallas to his friends and soldiers, x. 515. Of Jupiter to Juno, x. 856. Of Æneas to his friends, ii. 21. Of Æneas to the ambassadors from Laurentum, xi. 161. Of Latinus to Turnus, xii. 31. Of Æneas to Ascanius, xii. 644. Of Æneas to his army, xii. 825. Of Juturna to Turnus, xii 912. Of Jupiter to Juno, xii. 1147, 1205.

In the Supplicatory kind.

Juno's request to Æolus, i. 97. Of Venus to Jupiter, i. 314. Of Æneas to Venus, i. 450. Of Ilioneus to Dido, i. 734. Dido's invocation of Jupiter, i. 1020. Of Æneas to Dido, iv. 483. Of Dido to Anna, iv. 601. Of Æneas to Jupiter, v. 901. Of Venus to Neptune, v. 1020. Of Æneas to Apollo and the Sibyl, vi. 88. To the Sibyl, vi. 155. To the shade of Palinurus, vi. 167. Of Latinus to the Trojans, vii. 270. Of Amata to Latinus, vii. 501. Of Venus to Vulcan, viii. 492. Of Euryalus to Nisus, ix. 256. Of Nisus to the council, ix. 305. Of Ascanius to Nisus and Euryalus, ix. 339. Of Venus to Jupiter, x. 26. Of Cymodoce, the Nereid, to Æneas, x. 324. Of Magus to Æneas, x. 728. Of Turnus to Jupiter, x. 943. The petition of Aruns to Apollo, xi. 1153. Of Amata to Turnus, xii. 88. Of Juno to Juturna, xii. 216. Of Juno to Jupiter, xii 1177.

In the Vituperative kind.

Of Neptune to the winds, i. 88. Of Dido to Æneas, iv 441, 522. Of Numanus to the Trojans, ix. 811. Of Pandarus to Turnus, ix. 995. Mnestheus to the

SPEECHES.

Trojans, ix. 1054. Of Juno to Venus, x. 95. Of
Drances in the Council, xi, 519. Of Turnus in the
Council in anfwer to Drances, xi. 585. Of Tarchon
to the Trojans, xi. 1077. Of Juturna to the Rutu-
lians, xii. 346. Of Æneas to the Trojans, xii. 473.
Of Turnus to Juturna, xii. 918.

In the Complimentary, or Congratulatory kind.

Speech of Dido to the Trojans, i. 790. Of Æneas to
Dido, i. 834. Of Dido to Æneas, i. 870. Of
Æneas to his people, v. 59. Of Neptune to Venus,
v. 1045. Of Latinus to the Trojans, vii. 354. Of
Evander to Æneas, viii. 205. Of Vulcan to Venus,
viii. 523. Of Drances to Æneas, xi. 187. Of Turnus to Camilla, ii. 769.

In the Narrative.

Jupiter's fpeech to Venus, i. 350. Of Venus to Æneas,
i. 465. Of Æneas to Venus, i. 513. Æneas's re-
lation of the deftruction of Troy, to Dido, B. ii. & iii.
Of Dido to Anna, iv. 694. The declaration of the
Sibyl, vi. 129. Of the Sibyl to Æneas, vi. 441. Of
Ilioneus to Latinus, vii. 290. Of Æneas to Pallas,
viii. 154. Of Æneas to Evander, viii. 168. Of
Evander to Æneas, viii. 246. Of Venulus in the
council, ii. 372. Diana's relation of the ftory of
Camilla, ii. 815. Of Sages to Turnus, xii. 945.

In the Pathetick.

Of Æneas to Venus, i. 563. Of Dido to Anna, iv. 11.
Of Anna to Dido, iv. 42. Dido's laft fpeech, iv.
937. Of Æneas to the Ghoft of Anchifes, v. 106.
VOL. IV.   X

POETICAL INDEX.

SPEECHES.

Of Evander to Æneas, viii. 742. Nisus to Euryalus, ix. 266. Euryalus to Ascanius, ix. 373. Of Æneas over the dead body of Pallas, xi. 59. Of Evander over the dead body of Pallas, xi. 230.

In the Irony, or Sarcasm.

Of Juno to Venus, iv. 134. Of Venus to Juno, iv. 151.

Speech to an Horse.

Of Mezentius to his Horse Rhœbus, x. 1231.

DESCRIPTIONS of IMAGES.

A COLLECTION of the most remarkable throughout the ÆNEIS.

Descriptions of PLACES.

Of the building of Carthage, i. 586, &c.
Cave of Æolus, i. 78
———— the Sibyl, vi. 62.
Gate of Hell, vi. 384.
Palace of Laurentum, vii. 229.
———————— Pluto, vi. 857.

DESCRIPTIONS.

Paſſage to the Shades below, vi. 338.
Port (African) where Æneas and the Trojans landed,
   i 228.
Shades below, vi. 575, &c.
Temple of Appollo at Cumæ, vi. 17.
——————— Ceres, near Troy, ii. 969.
——————— Juno, at Carthage, i. 625.
Tomb of Dercennus, xi. 1235.
——————— Miſenus, vi. 332.

Deſcriptions of PERSONS.

Æneas, his beautiful countenance, &c. i. 824. Stand-
   ing over Turnus after he had wounded him, xii. 1360.
Apollo, on a golden Cloud encouraging Aſcanius to
   glory, ix. 873. Aſſuming the form of old Butes, ix.
   884.
Aſcanius, graceful, iv. 200. A bold hunter, iv. 223.
   Heading a troop of horſe at the games in honour of
   Anchiſes, v. 744. Hunting the ſtag, vii. 691. In-
   voking Jupiter, ix. 855. His beauty, x. 199.
Atis, beautiful, v. 741.
Aventinus, his ſhield and perſon, vii. 910. His origin,
   vii 914.
Bitias, gigantic, ix. 951.
Camilla, her appearance and valour, xi. 962. Her
   death, xi. 1203.
Charon, vi. 414.
Cupid, in appearance a boy, i. 960. Perſonates Iülus,
   i. 967, 889.
Cyclops, forged the gate and iron arch of the palace of
   Pluto, vi. 857. Their abode, viii. 551. Forge the
   armour of Æneas by command of Vulcan, viii. 553.
Dares, athletick, v. 486. Engages with Entellus, v.
   566. Is vanquiſhed, v. 624.
Diana, i. 700.

DESCRIPTIONS.

DESCRIPTIONS.

Turnus, defcribed in various fituations, from B. vii. to the end of tne Poem.

Venus, defcribed as an huntrefs, i. 435. As the Goddefs of Love, i. 556. Beautiful in all her appearances through the Poem.

Defcriptions of THINGS.

Abode of Alecto, vii. 777.

Battle, between the Harpies and the Trojans, iii. 313. *See the article* MILITARY Defcriptions.

Bowl, i. 1017.

Building, of Carthage, i. 586. Of the Temple of Juno, at Carthage, i. 626.

Burial, of the flain in battle, xi. 284.

Burning, of Troy, ii. 397, &c. Of the Trojan fleet, v. 889.

Ceremonies, at a feaft in honour of Hercules, viii. 371.

Chariot, driven and dividing a crowd, x. 620.

Council, of ftate, xi 362.

Crefts, waving, ix. 923.

Crowd, rufhing to pafs the Stygian ferry, vi. 422.

Cyclops, forging the armour of Æneas, viii. 583.

Death, of Dido, iv. 951. Of Rhemus, ix. 445. Of Bitias, ix. 959. Of Pandarus, ix. 1015. Of Mezentius, x. 1293, &c. Of Camilla, xi. 1203. Of Turnus, xii. 1376. *The Defcriptions of different forts of death in the Æneis, are innumerable, and fcattered throughout the battles.*

Defcent, of Mercury, i. 412. Of the Dira, xii. 1239.

Drefs of Chloreus, xi. 1136

Earth, (the) labouring under the tread of Heroes rufhing to battle, xii. 658.

Entertainment, one given by Dido to Æneas and the Trojans, i. 900—981.

X 3

POETICAL INDEX.

DESCRIPTIONS

Funeral pile, of Dido, iv. 727. Of Mifenus, vi. 308.
—— bier, xi. 95.
—— proceffion, xi. 90.
Game, a naval one, v. 151.
Hand, fevered from the body, holding a fauchion, x. 553.
Herd of ftags, i. 260.
Heroes, attending to ratify a peace, xii. 245, &c.
Horfes, of war; *innumerable defcriptions may be feen in the battles.*
Horfe, (wooden) that conftructed by the Greeks for the deftruction of Troy, defcribed, ii. 19.
—— of Æneas, viii. 730. Of Turnus, ix. 54. Of Mezentius, x. 1226. Knelt to receive his mafter, x 1241. Wounded, the effects, x. 1279. Of Pallas, at the funeral proceffion of his mafter, xi. 134. Chariot horfes of Turnus, xii. 127. Tofs their heads and neigh at his approach, xii. 123.
—— white, x 811.
—— of young Priam, v. 739.
Illumination, of the palace of Dido, i. 1015.
Images in the palace of Laurentum, vii, 241.
Leaping from a chariot, x. 636.
Mount Ætna defcribed, iii. 748.
Neptune's riding on the fea, v. 1069.
Oak-tree, ftripped of its boughs to erect a trophy with the fpoils of Mezentius, xi. 6.
Overthrow of Cacus, viii. 285.
Prefents made to Dido, i. 915.
Screech owl, iv. 672.
Of a facrifice, iv. 736. Of one to Juno, iv. 81. One on the ratification of peace, xii. 255. Sacrifices to particular deities, iii. 162.
Sinking part of the Trojan fleet in the ftorm, i. 154.
Stern, of Æneas's fhip, x. 232. Of another fhip, x. 250.

DESCRIPTIONS.

Stone, rolled down on the foe, ix. 773. Stone thrown by a hero, x. 192, 988. One heaved by Turnus, xii. 1300.

Storm, raifed by Æolus, i. 124, 148. One raifed by Juno, iv 231.

Trophy, one raifed by Æneas with the fpoils of Mezentius, xi. 6.

Veft, one given to Cloanthus, for conquering in the naval game, v. 325. Of two vefts, xi. 103.

Defcriptions, of TIMES *and* SEASONS.

Morning, iv. 7, 840. vii. 34. ix. 610 xii. 173.
Night, iii. 764. viii. 40, 484.
Dead of night, iv. 757.
Midnight, viii. 539.

MILITARY *Defcriptions.*

Armies, burying the flain in battle, xi. 284.
——— engaging, xii. 673.
——— broken, unite and join again in battle, xii. 104.
Armour, and veftment of Pallas, viii. 776. Of Æneas, viii. 821.
——— glittering, ix. 791.
——— of Turnus, ix. 990.
——— fcaled with gold, x. 434.
Army, on a march, viii. 772, 786.
——— approaching the walls of a town, xi. 898.
——— in confufion on the lofs of a leader, xi. 1257.
Arrow, hiffing through the air, ix. 866.
Arrows (Scythian) fwift of flight, viii 287.
Battle, left unfinifhed for a fingle combat, xii. 1012. Confufion of Battle, xi. 944. Day of Battle, xi. 901.
Belt, inlaid with gold, x. 691.

DESCRIPTIONS.

DESCRIPTIONS.

Descriptions of the INTERNAL PASSIONS, or their
VISIBLE EFFECTS.

POETICAL INDEX.

SIMILIES.

From Beasts.

The rage of Wolves in search of prey for their young, to the despair and fury of the Inhabitants of a city sacked by an enemy, ii. 479. The rage of a wounded hind, to that of Dido inflamed by desire, iii. 95. The roaming of a Wolf at night for prey, to the fury of Turnus searching for the Trojans, ix. 66. A Stag bounding against hounds and huntsmen, when encompassed by them, to the resolution of a soldier surrounded by his enemies, ix. 739. A Boar surrounded by huntsmen, to a General encompassed by revolting soldiers, x. 1000. A Courser freed from his keeper, and the restraint of reins, to Turnus descending from the Tower of Laurentum armed to battle, xi. 743. A Wolf flying, having only torn his prey, to Aruns flying after he had wounded Camilla, xi. 1183. The fleetness horses, to the flight of northern winds, xii. 133. The fury of the Bull, in fight of his female, to the raving of Turnus, xii. 159. A battle between two Bulls, to the combat between Æneas and Turnus, xii. 1042. A stag pursued by hounds, to Turnus pursued in flight by Æneas, xii. 1083.

From Lions.

The rage of a famished Lion, seeking prey, to the fury of Euryalus slaughtering the enemy, ix. 460. A Lion surrounded by the spears of hunters, to Turnus surrounded by the Trojans, ix. 1072. A Lion rushing on a Bull, to Turnus rushing on Pallas, x. 638. A lion rushing on a goat, or stag, to Mezentius rushing on his foes, x. 1026. The rage of a wounded lion, to the fury of Turnus, xii. 9.

SIMILIES.

From Birds.

The violence of an Eagle feizing its prey, to the anger of Pallas, i. 66. The joining of a flight of Swans after being purfued by an Eagle, to the meeting of the Trojan ihips after their feparation in the ftorm, i. 552. A frightened Dove leaving her neft and flying to the fhip of Mneftheus in the naval game, v. 276. An Eagle feizing its prey, to Turnus feizing Lycus, ix. 716. The rifing of Cranes before fouthern ftorms, to the army roufed by the appearance of Æneas, x. 370. A fwallow and hawk feeking food for their young, to the fury of Juturna driving the chariot of Turnus round the field of battle, xii. 691.

From Snakes.

The vauntings of Pyrrhus, and the glittering of his arms, to a fnake having renewed its fkin after winter, ii. 641. A fnake crufhed by the wheels of a carriage, to Sergefthus' fhattered veffel, v. 239. A Serpent feized by an Eagle, to the ftruggling of a prifoner taken by an enemy, ii. 1105.

From Fires.

The firing of weeds in Summer, to the renewal of vigour in the troops of Pallas, x. 566. Fire catching both fides of a wood, to the rage of different heroes in the field of battle, xii. 760.

From Trees.

An oak refifting winds, to Æneas withftanding the folicitations of Dido, iv. 640. The falling of a hollow

POETICAL INDEX.

SIMILIES.

pine, to Entellus falling in the gauntlet-fight, v. 599.
The height of fir-trees, to the gigantic height of
Bitias and Pandarus, ix. 917. Oak-trees overloaded,
and shook by winds, to their waving crests, ix. 924.

From FISH.

Dolphins chasing one another, to the turns and returns
of the Trojan youths at the warlike games, v. 775.

From WINDS.

Unfledged Winds, to the murmurs and mixed applause
in the council of the Gods, x. 149. The contention
of winds, to the contention of two armies, x. 496.
The fury of raging Boreas, to the fury of Turnus,
xii. 542.

From STARS and COMETS.

The transcendency of the Morning star, over the rest,
to the superior appearance of Pallas, over others, viii.
778. The sanguine streams of Comets, to the defects
of the lustre of Æneas's shield, x. 380. Orion stalk-
ing over the flood, to Mezentius towering amidst his
troops, x. 1084.

From the SUN and MOON.

The reflection of the Sun, or Moon, on polished brass,
to an anxious and distressed mind, viii. 34.

From STORMS and TORRENTS.

The increase of a storm, to the increasing fury of a
battle, vii. 736. Storm of the elements, to the Storm
of a battle, ix. 908. Storms rending the skies, and

SIMILIES.

torrents the earth, to Æneas raging in battle, x. 850.
Rapid torrents falling from rocks, to the rage of two
heroes fcouring the field of battle.

From the SEA.

The flux and reflux of furges on the fhore, to the flight
and return of an army, xi. 929.

SIMILIES, exalting the characters of Men, by comparing them to GODS.

Neptune calming a ftormy fea, to a pious man quelling
a tumult, i. 213. Diana compared to Dido, i. 707.
Apollo in all his glory to Æneas, iv. 204. The fury
and magnanimity of the God of war, to that of
Turnus, xii. 499.

MISCELLANEOUS SIMILIES.

Polifhed Ivory, or Parian Marble, chafed with gold, to
the beauty of Æneas, i. 830. The fwarming of
Bees, to the iffuing of troops from a City, ii. 34.
The contention of winds to the renewal of a fight, ii.
565. Boys whipping a top, to the fury of Amata, vii.
528. A boiling cauldron, to the fury of Turnus, vii.
645. A rock incapable of being moved, to the fta-
bility of Latinus, vii. 809. The mountains Atlas
and Appenine, to the greatnefs of Æneas, xii. 1020.

INDEX

OF

ARTS AND SCIENCES.

BY MR. POTTER.

N.B. *The first number marks the Book, the second the Verse.*

ARTS MILITARY.

AMBASSADORS soliciting a truce of peace, xi. 149.
Armour-bearer, ix. 442.

Army, marching in silence and discipline, ix. 29. Incamped before a city, ix. 199.

———— Laying before a city at night, ix. 207. Asleep after a debauch, ix. 423. Repulsed by poles, and missive weapons, ix. 677.

Attack (general) x. 429.

Battle, between the Latian peasants and the Trojans, vii. 725. Suspension of a battle on the approach of night, xi. 1316.

Bulwarks, the approach of an enemy observed from them, ix. 46.

Charioteer, ix. 443.

City, in danger of being besieged, ix. 211. What works necessary, ix. 213.

Combat, (single) x. 667. xii. 1035.

General, animating his soldiers with courage, ix. 616.

Ignoble, to pursue the enemy flying, xii. 683.

Landing troops, x. 402.

Marshalling an army, xi. 703.

Military exercises, ix. 673.

Olive branches, signs of peace, xi. 150, 505.

Palisades, ix. 694.

Plundering the slain, ix. 485.

Scaling walls, with ladders, ix. 713.

Scouts, xi. 684. Bringing intelligence to the General, xii. 945.

RURAL ARTS.

ARCHITECTURE.

ASTRONOMY.

DIVINATION and AUGURY.

GYMNASTICKS.

Racing, on foot, v. 415.
Gauntlet-fight, v. 566.

GEOGRAPHY.

A Table of those places whose situation, products, people, or history, &c. are mentioned in the Æneis. The whole being properly illustrated.

Abella, a town of Campania, in Italy, vii. 1020.
Æthiopian climates, their situation, iv. 696.
Ætna, the mount, by what known, iii. 728.
Agragas, crowned with lofty summits, iii. 924, famous for producing warlike Steeds, 925.
Albano, the mount, xii. 205.
Albula, the river Tiber once so called, viii. 439.
Albunea, the river, sulphureous, vii. 124.
Allia, the river, vii. 993.
Amasene, the river, vii 947. xi. 825.
Amsanctus, the lake, its situation, vii. 777.
Anagnia, the chief city of the Hernici, vii 947.
Angitian woods, near the Fucine lake in Italy, vii. 1041.
Anien, a river of Italy, vii. 945.
Antandros, a city of Phrygia, iii. 7.
Antemnæ, a city of the Sabines, vii. 872.
Appenine, the mountain or ridge of hills, parting Italy, through the middle, from the Alps, xii. 1021.
Arcadian land, a country in Peloponnesus, or the Morea, viii. 70.
Ardua, once a famous city of Latium, where *Turnus* kept his court, built by *Danaë*, now called Ardea, vii. 576.
Argos, a city of Peloponnesus, ii. 446. vi. 1151. vii. 396.
Argyripa, a town of Apulia, built by Diomedes, xi. 377.
Arisba, once a city, near Abydos and Lampsacum, ix. 350.
Asia's lakes, vii. 968.
Asium, a city of Spoleto, in Italy, x. 247.
Athos, a mountain of Macedon, xii. 1020.
Atlas, a high hill in Mauritania, crowned with piny forests, iv. 362.
Avernus, a lake of Campania, in Italy, the water of which is black, iii. 562.

Geloan fields, belonging to the river, and city Gela, in Sicily, iii. 922.

Getulia's barren fands, v. 67.

Getulian cities, *i. e.* cities of Getulia, a country of Africk near the Syrtes, iii. 56.

Gnofian Shore; belonging to Gnofius, or Crete, iii. 157.

Gravifca, an ancient city of Tufcany, now called Corneto, x. 263.

Hermus, a river of Lydia, faid to have golden fands, vii. 996.

Hernicus, rocky, vii. 946.

Hefperia, the ancient name given to Italy, i. 748. iii. 221.

Hefperia's Plains, rich, vii. 5.

Himella, a river of the Sabines, ix. 987.

Janicula's remains, the ruins of a fort, on a hill adjoining to Rome, viii. 469.

Ida, a famous hill, or mount, in Phrygia, near Troy, iii. 7. ix. 93.

Idalian bowers; belonging to Idalia, a mountain of Crete, facred to Venus, i. 955.

Ilva, an Ifland of the Tyrrhene fea, oppofite Tufcany, x. 253.

India, in the general, a large country of Afia, vi. 1082.

Ifmarus, a mountain of Thrace, towards the Archipelago, x. 488.

Italy; a moft delightful and fruitful country; once called *Hefperia,* from its weftern fituation, i. 103. See *Hefperia.*

Ithaca, a country of Ionia, iii. 353.

Latium, a country of Italy, famous for the War celebrated in the *Æneis,* i. 286. xii. 1201.

Laurentum, (the city of *King Latinus,* near Lavinium in Italy) from whence its name, vii. 93. Famous for its lofty Towers, x. 948.

Lerna's lake, near Argos in Peloponnefus, xii. 754.

Leucate, a very high ridge on the promontory Leucas, famous for a temple dedicated to Apollo, iii. 355.

Libyan fhores, belonging to Libya, i. 227.

Lilybean Strand, belonging to the promontory Lilybœum, in Sicily, dangerous from its rocks and moving fand, iii. 927.

Lipare, an Iſle near Sicily, principal of the Ætolian, viii. 552.

Lydia, a plenteous inland country of Aſia Minor, x. 209.

Lyrneſſus, a town of Troas, in Phrygia, xii. 800.

Mæotian lake, beyond the Euxine ſea, vi. 1088.

Malæan flood, the ſea encompaſſing the promontory Maʾéa, dangerous to Mariners, v. 251.

Mantua, a famous city of Italy, near Cremona, but beyond the Po, named after Manto, celebrated for being the place of *Virgil*'s nativity, x. 288.

Nar, a river of Umbria, in Italy, of a ſulphureous quality, vii. 720.

Naxos, one of the Cyclade Iſles, famous for good wines, iii. 171.

Neritos, a rocky Iſle in the Ionian ſea, iii. 352.

Numician ſtreams, *i. e.* the river Numicus, in Italy, vii. 1089.

Nurſia, the fartheſt northern City of the Sabines, vii. 1027.

Pachynus, a promontory of Sicily, iii. 548. Its ſhore rocky. 918. lofty, vii. 395.

Pactolus, a river in Lydia, ſaid to have golden ſands, x. 211.

Padua, an ancient Venetian city, built by Antenor, i. 336.

Palanteum, a city of Italy, built by Pallas, the grandfather of King Evander, viii. 73.

Pantagias, a ſmall, rapid river of Sicily, rocky at its entrance, iii. 903.

Paros, one of the Cyclade Iſles, famous for quarries of white marble, iii. 173.

Pelorus, a promontory of Sicily, iii. 525, 902.

Petilia, a town of Magna Græcia, built on a mountain, by Philoctetes, iii. 515.

Phrygian ſea, i. 527. Fields, ii. 791. Shore, iv. 860.

Piemmyrium's watry ſtrand, iii. 908.

Po, a river of Piedmont, in Italy, vi. 893.

Pomptina, once a very conſiderable lake in Campania, vii. 1093

Preneſte, a city of Italy, near Rome, viii. 743.

Privernum, a town of the Volſcians in Italy, xi. 816.

Prochyta, a small Island in the Tyrrhenian sea, ix. 968.

Rhætean Shores, belonging to the country of the Grisons, on the Alps, iii. 148.

Rocks of Scylla, i. 279. See Scylla.

Rome, the chief city of Italy, and once of the world; renowned for a succession of glory, i. 10. Celebrated for its lofty towers, vi. 1065.

Sabine land, i. e. belonging to the Sabines, a very ancient and famous people of Italy, vii. 125.

Salamis, a city in Cyprus, built by Teucer, i. 877.

Salentinian fields, i. e. belonging to the Salentines, or Magna Græcia, iii. 514.

Sarnus, a river of Italy, which has its source on the Mountain Sarus, and passing through Campania reaches as far as the bay of Naples, vii. 1019.

Saturnia's Gabine land, i. e. belonging to the Gabii, a town of the Volscians, patronized by Juno, vii. 944.

————— Remains, i. e. the ruins of Saturnia, a very ancient city of Italy, viii. 469.

Scæan Gate, a Gate of the City of Troy, ii. 830.

Scylacæan strands, belonging to Scylaceum, a city on the coast of Sicily, iii. 726.

Scylla, (the rock) its situation, iii. 536.

Selinus, a town of Cilicia, on a river of the same name, iii. 926.

Sicilian Shores, belonging to the Island of Sicily, i. 51.

Sicily, an island between Africk and Italy, iii. 524, v. 34.

Sidician Shores, i. e. belonging to Sidicinum Teanum, a city of Campania, vii. 1007.

Simois, a river flowing from Mount Ida by Troy, xi. 395.

Strophades, (the islands) their situation, &c. iii. 274.

Stygian lake; the river Styx, vi. 503.

Syrtes, two quicksands, in the farthest part of Africa, iii. 59. vii. 418.

Tarentum's bay, belonging to a very ancient city of Calabria, iii. 723.

Tarpeian rock, mount Tarpejus, viii. 457.

Tenedos, the isle, its situation near Troy, ii. 27.

Tetrica, a mountain in the North of Italy, vii. 985.

HISTORY.

Of Hippolytus, vii. 1049. Of the overthrow of Cacus, viii. 285. Of the actions of Hercules, viii. 383. Of Camilla, xi. 815.

MUSIC.

Cymbals used by Cybele, in the Idean woods, iii. 153.
Trumpet, used to give the signal for war, viii. 4.
Trumpets wake the lazy war, viii. 574. ix. 667.
————— sounding hoarsely in a funeral procession, xi. 137.
Drums and trumpets, found mournfully at funerals, xi. 293.

MECHANICKS.

Armoury and Instruments of War.] See the Military Descriptions.
Swords and Bucklers made of brass, by whom used, vii. 1022.
Dart, thrown in sign of war, ix. 60.
Bow, ix. 804. Apollo's bow, ix. 900.

ORATORY.
See the article Speeches, *in the Poetical Index.*

POLICY.

Kings.] Supreme in councils of the state, xi. 366. Not absolutely independent of the councils, xi. 463. 508.
Peace.] Ratified by the oaths of monarchs, xii. 266, &c.

SURGERY.

Iäpis dressing the wound of Æneas, xii. 587. The wound cured by the interposition of Venus, xii. 609.

PAINTING, SCULPTURE, &c.
See the Shield of *Æneas*, Book viii.

Characters of Grace.] The majesty and grace of the celestial deities, superior to that of men, throughout the Poem. Of grace in Ascanius, iv. 200. God-like grace in Turnus, xi. 740. Graceful mein of Camilla, xi. 755.
Characters of Beauty.] Beauty of countenance in Æneas, i. 824. Beauty of a young man, in Euryalus, v. 387. In Atis, v. 741. In Ascanius, v. 744. x. 199 In Lausus, vii. 899. In Pallas, x. 614. In Camers and Numa, x. 787. Of an old man in Latinus, vii. 68. Beauty of eyes, in Juno, x. 862. Beauty of complexion in La-

vinia, xii. 101, 886. Venus reprefented beautiful in every fituation throughout the Poem.

Largenefs of Body.] See the Defcriptions of Bitias, Entellus, and Pandarus. Largenefs of limbs, in Theron, x. 432. Of Bulk, in Gyas, x. 442. Brawny thighs of Turnus, xi. 735.

For pictures of particular Things, fee the article Images *in the Poetical Index.*

Hiftory, &c. in the Shield of Æneas, Book viii.

Sculpture and Carving.] See the defcription of the ftatues in the palace of Laurentum, vii. 243, &c.

Two carved Lions, x. 233.

Helm of Cupavo, x. 268.

Statue of Apollo, x. 250.

Stern of a fhip, x. 280.

POETRY.
See the intire Index.

THEOLOGY.

A View of the SYSTEM, *fupported by* VIRGIL.

JUPITER, *or the fupreme Being,* fuperior to all the other powers of heaven, x. 1, 153.

All human affairs governed by fate, x. 615. Fate certain, and therefore not to be feared, x. 631. The fhortnefs of life only lengthened by Virtue, x. 658. Fate irrefiftible, x. 662. The will of Jupiter is fate, x. 665. The Gods attend to human affairs, x. 1075.

The inferior Deities, have different offices under God; fee their defcriptions and employs, in the different tables.

The Doctrine of rewards and punifhments, after death, is forcibly inculcated in the defcriptions of the fhades below; fee Book vi.

Æneas, the Hero of the Poem, is drawn a pious Prince, yielding all to the Gods, and frequently ufing Prayer; which is recommended on all enterprizes throughout the *Æneis.*

F I N I S.

www.ingramcontent.com/pod-product-compliance
Lightning Source LLC
Chambersburg PA
CBHW030858270326
41929CB00008B/475